MORE
THAN
WORDS

vocabulary for upper intermediate to advanced students

BOOK 1

 LONGMAN

Addison Wesley Longman Limited
Edinburgh Gate, Harlow,
Essex CM20 2JE, England
and Associated companies throughout the world

First published 1991

Set in 11/13pt Futura Medium

Designed and produced by
The Pen and Ink Book Company Ltd.
Huntingdon, Cambridgeshire

Illustrated by Maureen and Gordon Gray,
Hamish Moyle, Dave Parkins and John York

Fifth impression 1997

British Library Cataloguing in Publication Data
Harmer, Jeremy, *1947—*
    More than words: vocabulary for upper intermediate to
    advanced students.
    Book 1.
    I. Title II. Rossner, R. (Richard)
    428.1
Printed in China
EPC/05

ISBN 0-582-09481-X

|2| *Related and unrelated meanings*

SAME WORD, DIFFERENT MEANINGS

One of the first things people notice about English words is that the same word can have different meanings depending on the context in which it is used.

1 How many different meanings can you think of for each of the following words? Write a brief example sentence for each meaning, and compare your examples with a partner's.

> can book flat right left line like

Can you think of words that have more than one meaning in your own language?

2 Read the following text. What kind of book or article do you think it was taken from?

3 Answer these questions:

a How had the patient changed in the time between being admitted and the nurse's phone call?

b How do you think the story will continue?

4 For each of these words, find at least one meaning which is different from the meaning they have in the text.

> singular patient admitted second
> carrying on   floor

The man who fell out of bed

When I was a medical student many years ago, one of the nurses called me in considerable perplexity, and gave me this singular story on the phone. They had a new patient − a young man − just admitted that morning. He had seemed very nice, very normal, all day − until a few seconds before when he awoke from a snooze. He then seemed excited and strange − not himself in the least. He had somehow contrived to fall out of bed, and was now sitting on the floor, carrying on and vociferating, and refusing to go back to bed. Could I come, please, and sort out what was happening?

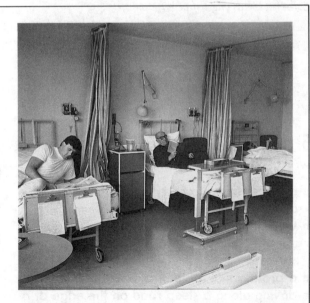

6 Related and unrelated meanings

ACTIVATE
5 Now use the same words to complete the following:

a After the police had questioned him for twelve hours, Jones finally _____ that he had planted the bomb under the Minister's car. The police had arrested him as he was leaving his flat on the third _____ of a run-down building in South London. But he had escaped from the police station where he was being held. Jones was arrested a __Second__ time just as he was boarding a plane bound for New York.

b A: Is 'criteria' _____ or plural?
  B: Plural, I think.
  A: What's the _____ form, then?
  B: I don't know. Look it up.

c Mr Thomas, who is not a _____ man at the best of times, flew into a rage when he heard that the train to Cardiff had been cancelled, and that he would have to wait an hour and a half for the next one.

d It's highly unlikely that anyone will ever run 100 metres in under nine _____.

*Sometimes the different meanings of a word are related. For example, a **fishing line**, a **clothes line** and a **line** drawn on a sheet of paper are all different things but with something in common – they are all long and narrow.*

6 Find different but related meanings for the word DROP in the following situations:

a a waiter trying to carry a tray full of plates and dishes
b walking in the rain
c using a plane to get food to starving people in Africa
d a professional football or basketball team
e driving along a steep road on the edge of a mountain

*Sometimes the different meanings are not related: e.g. **bear** (the animal) has nothing to do with **I can't bear the pain**. They are, in a way, different words.*

7 Find different and unrelated meanings for these words in the situations indicated:

a lie   – someone with an illness
        – someone being interviewed by police

b row   – a classroom
        – a boat

c racket – a party
         – a sport
         – criminal activity

d stick – making a model car
        – an old person going for a walk

e tip   – a meal in a restaurant
        – someone asking for advice before doing something for the first time
        – someone trying to remember a word
        – an accident while having a drink

ACTIVATE
8 Use at least two of the words from exercise 7 to write a short dialogue about one of the situations above.

SETS OF WORDS

> Words can often be grouped together in 'sets' with related meanings. For example, there are many words that are related to cooking, such as *fry, boil, saucepan, knife, etc.*

9 Organize this group of words and expressions into *three* different families. Show your lists to a partner and explain why you have grouped the words in the way you have.

> amusement   patient   tests
> fall asleep   joke   neurologist   wake up
> sense of humour   bedclothes   dissect

10 Read the continuation of the text. List words from the text which have meanings related to:

a *surprise* or *shock*
b *dislike*

ACTIVATE

11 Ask a partner what she or he thinks happened or is happening to the young man in the text. Think how you would have felt in the young man's situation, and complete these expressions:

I would have felt_____
I would have found the experience_____
_____

Then, together, look at the words you have used, and the words used in the text to describe the young man's feelings, and try to organize them in a table like this:

Related to:	-ed adjectives	-ing adjectives
Fear	e.g. frightened	frightening
Amusement		
Surprise		
Confusion		

The man who fell out of bed (Continued)

When I arrived I found the patient lying on the floor by his bed and staring at one leg. His expression contained anger, alarm, bewilderment and amusement — bewilderment most of all, with a hint of consternation. I asked him if he would go back to bed, or if he needed help, but he seemed upset by these suggestions and shook his head. I squatted down beside him, and took the history on the floor. He had come in that morning for some tests, he said. He had no complaints, but the neurologists, feeling he had a 'lazy' left leg, thought he should come in. He had felt fine all day, and fallen asleep towards evening. When he woke up he felt fine too, until he moved in bed. Then he found, as he put it, 'someone's leg' in the bed — a severed human leg, a horrible thing! He was stunned, at first, with amazement and disgust — he had never experienced, never imagined, such an incredible thing. He felt the leg gingerly. It seemed perfectly formed, but 'peculiar' and cold. At this point he had a brainwave. He now realised what had happened: it was all a joke! A rather monstrous and improper but very original joke! It was New Year's Eve, and everyone was celebrating. Obviously, one of the nurses with a macabre sense of humour had stolen into the Dissecting Room and nabbed a leg, and slipped it under his bedclothes as a joke when he was fast asleep. But when he threw it out of bed, he somehow came after it — and now it was attached to him!

Oliver Sacks *The Man who Mistook his Wife for a Hat* (Picador)

📖**12** The author says the man also felt angry. Here are three words meaning *angry*. Put them in order from the most angry to the least angry:

angry   furious   annoyed

LEAST _____ MOST

Now organize the words you have put in the table in exercise 11 in the same way.

ACTIVATE

13 Use adjectives ending in *-ed* and *-ing*, such as exciting and excited, and other adjectives, to describe how you felt during a very enjoyable experience you've had in the last two years: for example, a holiday, or show or sporting event you went to, a reunion or party, a marriage or birth in the family, etc.

14 The author of this text is a doctor. What do you think he said to the young man after listening to his story?

Sense relations

GENERAL AND SPECIFIC

Sometimes pairs or groups of words can be related in meaning and belong to the same 'family', but one is more 'general' in meaning than the other(s).

1 In each of the following exchanges the words *in italics* belong to the same family. Write these words in the correct columns beside each exchange.

	Most general	More specific	Most specific
Example: 'Would you like some *fruit*?' 'Yes, please. Can I have an *apple*?'	fruit	apple	
a) 'I'll just *boil* this pasta.' 'It doesn't need much *cooking*, does it? It says on the packet: "Put in hot water and *simmer* for three minutes".'			
b) 'Oh Mummy! Look at that *bear*!' 'Oh yes. I think it's a *polar bear*. They're lovely *animals*.'			
c) 'Let's have a *drink*. Do you want a *lager*?' 'No, thanks. I don't like *beer*.'			
d) 'I saw her *walking* to College yesterday, *strolling* nonchalantly along Park Street.' 'Yes, she normally *goes* that way.'			

Using a mixture of both general and more specific words and expressions helps us to be clearer about what we mean and to avoid repeating the same words, thus making what we say or write more interesting.

2 Read this brief news item.

List the words that are used to refer to:
a the person involved
b the vehicle involved
c the damage to the vehicle

THERE WAS a serious accident on the M25 yesterday. A delivery van ran into the crash barrier and turned over. The vehicle was severely damaged, the windscreen was smashed, and the driver was badly injured. Police believe the man fell asleep at the wheel of his Ford Transit, which was a virtual write-off. The forty-five-year-old father of two was taken to Watford General Hospital with multiple fractures.

3 Replace the words underlined in the text with appropriate words from the box.

20 year-old bank clerk	woman
apologetic Mrs Castro	young man

A customer celebrating his birthday with friends was suddenly attacked by the proprietor of the Cossack Restaurant yesterday. The <u>customer</u> was taken by surprise when the <u>proprietor</u> broke a plate over his head. However, the <u>customer</u> agreed to let the matter drop when the <u>proprietor</u> explained that she had assaulted him because she had mistaken him for another person, who had thrown a plateful of spaghetti at her the night before.

4 In this text, put words from the lists below in the appropriate spaces.

cat	owner
Siamese	university professor
pet	animal lover
exhausted animal	save
mother of six	rescued
	bring to safety

A _____ was finally _____ from a well in Cambridge after a four-day battle to keep her alive. The _____ fell down the disused shaft on Thursday. The _____, who was alerted by a neighbour who heard loud miaows, immediately got to work to try to _____ his _____. With the help of friends the _____ began to dig away at the narrow opening while his children mounted a round-the-clock vigil, lowering food and milk to the _____ in a specially adapted bucket every few hours. It was only after special help from the fire brigade that the _____ was finally able to _____ the _____.

ACTIVATE

5 Imagine you want to tell a story about the following:

a a wild animal
b a criminal
c a building

List two more specific words or phrases that you could use in addition to each of these general terms when telling the story.
Then make up a very short story and tell it to a partner.

6 Work with a partner. Think up an imaginary (or real!) news item suitable for a local paper to go with one of these headlines. It should be 'light' but unusual, and will probably involve referring to the same people or things in different ways.

NEW CITY BUS GETS STUCK UNDER BRIDGE

Five-husband grandmother marries her sixth

Lost rabbit turns up at Post Office

Sometimes the meaning relation between two words is so close that they are very nearly SYNONYMS, that is, they have nearly equivalent meanings (e.g. **big** and **large**). However, it is rare that two words or expressions have exactly the **same** meaning: usually there is a difference of style, register, nuance, usage, etc. We use the different terms for a purpose, for example in order to avoid unnecessary repetition, or to give a different emphasis.

7 Find appropriate synonyms or near synonyms to complete the following exchanges as indicated. Do not repeat any of the words that A uses.

Example: A: What a glorious day!
B: Yes, lovely, isn't it.

a A: You look tired.
B: Yes, I'm _____.

b A: That film was awful, wasn't it.
B: Yes, _____.

c A: Look at that fool trying to overtake.
B: What _____!

d A: You must be very pleased with the result.
B: Yes, I'm _____.

e A: Did the hurricane damage your garden badly?
B: Yes, it _____ it.

f A: Wake up! You were dozing off.
B: Sorry, I didn't mean to _____.

OPPOSITES AND COUNTERPARTS

Within families of words, it is often possible to find pairs of opposites, especially with adjectives (e.g. **wide** and **narrow**). Finding pairs like this can be helpful when trying to remember vocabulary.

8 Find the opposites or counterparts for the words in the box. Then use each pair of words to describe two people or things.

strong evil ancient patient
decisive broad optimistic luxurious
impetuous exciting cool

9 Here are some expressions involving opposites. What do they mean?

blow hot and cold
in black and white
the long and the short of it
off and on
a love-hate relationship
back and forth

Use any three of these expressions in a brief love story with the title:

Absence makes the heart grow fonder

UNIT | 4 | *Metaphor, idioms, proverbs*

1 Using a dictionary, match the verbs to the correct pictures. Sometimes more than one word is possible.

> bark cackle grunt bleat
> squawk whinny hoot purr roar

a

b

c

d

e

f

g

h

i

2 In English we say that dogs go 'woof, woof' and cats go 'miaow, miaow'. What sounds do they make in your language?

*The meaning of the words in exercise 1 can be extended to apply to the way that we (humans) speak or react. This is an example of **metaphor**.*

3 Use some of the verbs to show how the person in each picture is speaking. Sometimes more than one answer is possible.

'Get your hair cut,' he _____.

'Hmmph! The country's going to the dogs' she _____.

'Get out of my house and don't come back', he _____.

'Another one for the basket', she _____.

'Ooh, that's funny', she _____.

'B-b-b-u-t I d-d-on't w-want to', he _____.

'A ghost? In my house? Eeeek!' he _____.

'I like it when you bring me presents', she _____.

ACTIVATE

4 Using words from exercises 1 and 3 describe what the people do in the following situations.

a A big man goes downstairs with a shotgun in the middle of the night and finds a young thief in the house.
b A witch captures a young child and puts him into the pot.
c Two young people find themselves lost in the fog in a churchyard in the middle of the night.
d A husband and wife are guests at a smart dinner party, but unfortunately they have a bit too much to drink.
e A teacher finds that two of her pupils have let down the tyres of her car, and sees them trying to run away.

5 Explain the following metaphors:

a It rained buckets.
b They woke to a carpet of snow over the land.
c The trees sighed in the breeze.

How do you describe weather in your language. What common metaphors do you use?

Sometimes a metaphor is continued for more than just one word or phrase.

6 Read the following poem and answer the questions.

a What is being described here?
b What do you think it is being compared to?

The wind clawed through the shrunken trees
And scratched and bit and roared with rage.
He felt the steam of hot breath on his face
Growling, loose-limbed. He stood, lashed
By the sting of its tail as it launched itself
Through the air away from him, ignored,
    Towards some other prey. He sinks,
    Now, to the quiet ground relieved
At the temporary calm, suddenly secure.

Peter Hedley

7 List six words or phrases from the poem which form part of the extended metaphor.

a _____
b _____
c _____
d _____
e _____
f _____

*Sometimes metaphors are used so often that they become fixed in the language as common phrases – or **idioms**.*

8 Look at the comments made by the people in the picture below. Match the idioms in italics with these sentences.

a Leave things as they are if by mentioning them again you are likely to cause problems.

b If the punishment is going to be equally bad for both bad and very bad behaviour, I'll behave very badly.

c The information came from somebody with first-hand knowledge.

d Don't waste time and effort by returning to an issue which has already been decided.

e It will cause trouble.

f The largest part of something.

g He likes teasing people.

h It will distinguish between the good and the bad.

DICTIONARY STUDY

📖 **9** Under which word would you find the following idioms in a dictionary?

a flog a dead horse
b one may as well be hanged for a sheep as for a lamb
c play cat and mouse with somebody
d let sleeping dogs lie

Look in a dictionary. Were you right?

> *Some idioms are only two words – often pairs of opposites, e.g.* **high and dry, touch and go.** *Some become phrasal verbs (see Part A Unit 11) and some are longer such as the ones in exercise 8. Generally the words and the order in idioms can not be changed.*

📖 **10** Using a dictionary say which of the following idiomatic expressions in italics are used correctly and correct those which are wrong.

a It was horrible watching her eat. She *made a real pig of herself.*
b *Pull up your horses.* Don't rush into this.
c His attitude to women is terrible. He's a real *male chauvinist ox.*
d While you're there can you call on Miss Njabella as well? You may as well *kill two birds with one bullet.*
e I'm not surprised they got on so well. *Birds of a feather,* you know...

ACTIVATE

11 Use one of the idioms from exercises 8–10 to comment on the following situations.

a Someone who has got a cold because of the weather.

b Someone who causes chaos by telling somebody something about their friend.
c Someone who realises they have been discovered stealing secrets from a company and goes on to do something even worse.
d Someone who tries to get local residents involved in a clean-up in the area despite local apathy.
e Someone who uses the opportunity of one visit to complete at least two overdue tasks.

> *All languages have 'wise sayings' or* **proverbs.** *These have become fixed phrases even though what they describe no longer exists, e.g.* **"don't put the cart before the horse"** *(× don't do things back to front) is still used although horses and carts are no longer used in Britain.*

📖 **12** Using a dictionary or any other source say what the following proverbs mean.

a A stitch in time saves nine.
b Better the devil you know than the one you don't.
c Don't put all your eggs in one basket.
d Two wrongs don't make a right.
e A bird in the hand is worth two in the bush.
f It takes two to tango.

Are there any equivalents to these proverbs in your own language? Translate proverbs from your own language into English.

ACTIVATE

13 Look for metaphorical use either in your own language or in English. Look at:
a advertisements   b poems   c stories

Say what is being described, and as what, as you did in exercise 6.

5 Collocation – which word goes with which?

It is often important to choose the right word to go with another word. For example, an adjective can be used to describe some nouns but not others. We can say **blonde woman** or **blond man** but not *blonde dog or *blonde horse! 'Blonde' does not **collocate** with dog or horse. Many words in the following groups are restricted in similar ways:

verbs and objects: we *drive a car* but we can't *drive a motorbike*.

subjects and verbs: *the telephone rang* but not *the telephone sounded*.

adjectives and prepositions: *full of* but not *full with*

verbs and prepositions: *arrive at* but not *arrive to*

verbs and adverbs: *I strongly believe* but not *I strongly think*.

1 Which of these verbs is commonly used with which object?

drive	your shoulders
ride	your homework
nod	a bus
shrug	your head
tell	your bed
say	a lie
make	this bicycle
do	a word in Russian

For each of these verbs, list three direct objects that can follow them.

drive tell say make do

2 Which of the combinations of adjectives and nouns below is unusual? Why? Suggest improvements where necessary.

a a fat piece of wood
b a wrong answer
c a strange coincidence
d a dead apple
e a fat dog
f a wrong mistake
g a touching letter
h a heavy drink
i a touching hand
j a heavy meal

For each of these adjectives, list two other nouns which can follow them.

heavy   strong   fat   thick

ACTIVATE

3 With a partner write a description of a very difficult but memorable imaginary journey lasting two days. Use the following words and ideas, as well as your own. Be careful to use appropriate verbs and adjectives with these words:

car breakdown the middle of nowhere lift lorry/truck driver/drinking accident ambulance hospital phone family disappeared

4 Which prepositions usually follow these adjectives?

interested _____ music
enthusiastic _____ the game
different _____ the bread we eat
keen _____ learning Spanish
late _____ her appointment with the
   doctor
afraid _____ large dogs
polite _____ his boss
disgusted _____ himself

Now for each of the following prepositions, list two other adjectives that could precede them:

about   for   with   of

5 Circle the best alternatives in this newspaper article.

List the words you have selected in the phrases below:

to _____ a campaign
to _____ a disease/epidemic
to reduce alcohol _____
to _____ awareness
it was agreed _____ them
_____ drinking/smoking
the death/birth _____ is high
a rich _____ of fatty foods/sugar
avoid exposure _____
a _____ diet

Anti-Cancer week backs healthy life

A CAMPAIGN telling people they can avoid cancer by healthy living was **started / launched/ set off** in London yesterday. Europe Against Cancer Week will involve a nationwide drive to **raise / lift / put up** public awareness of steps to **limit / control / manage** the disease. The code agreed **with / to / by** health ministers of the European Community Nations advises:

• Do not smoke. If you are already a smoker, you should try to give up or at least cut down on the number of cigarettes you smoke, and try not to smoke in other people's company.
• Reduce alcohol **consumption / intake / drinking. Serious / Bad / Heavy** drinking and smoking are associated with a high death **level / rate / amount** from cancer of the oesophagus.

• Avoid over-exposure **of / to / under** the sun.
• Adhere to safety procedures if handling cancer-inducing substances.
• Stick to a balanced, healthy **meal / food / diet**, concentrating on fresh fruit and vegetables, high fibre cereals, and a limited **consumption / eating / intake** of fatty foods.

6 Look at the list of recommendations in the campaign. Which three would be most difficult for you to comply with? List them in order of difficulty.

7 With a partner, work out a similar code for a 'World Happiness Week'.

8 One way to show collocation is on a grid like this:

	person	tree	building	mountain	fence
tall	✓	✓	✓	✗	✓
high	✗	✗	✓	✓	✓

Complete the grids below in a similar way:

	a story	something	in a quiet voice
speak			
say			
tell			

	a lie	French	yes or no	the truth
speak				
say				
tell				

ACTIVATE

9 Use any of these five words from exercise 8 to complete the sentences.

> *tall   high   speak   say   tell*

a The _____ man in the blue jacket was _____ the truth when he _____ this city was popular with tourists.

b Last night Jim _____ his little daughter a story about a prince who was kidnapped by a very _____ giant.

c There were only four or five journalists present, but the Prime Minister _____ in a very loud voice, as if she was addressing them from a _____ balcony.

d Julia _____ quite good Spanish and Portuguese.

e He never remembers to _____ 'please' and 'thank you'.

10 Think of three adjectives in your own language which must be followed by certain nouns, and two verbs which must be followed by certain objects. Use a dictionary to find out whether the collocation rules are the same for the equivalent words in English.

Style and register

1 The two dialogues below have got mixed up after the first line. Put them in the right order and then say what the difference between them is.

Hey, I love your coat! Where did you get it?

Can I have a proper look?

No, sorry.

Hang on . . . here you are. Hand-made, you know.

It's my sister's. Nice, isn't it?

Thanks. Wow, it's great! I don't suppose you know where she got it?

I'm sorry to bother you, but do you mind my asking where you bought that charming bag?

It's absolutely exquisite. Thank you so much for showing it to me.

Certainly. As you can see, it's hand-made.

Really? Could I possibly have a closer look?

Not at all. As a matter of fact, it was a present from a friend in India.

2 Why do you think people speak to certain other people formally? Put the numbers 0 (= not an important reason), 1, 2 or 3 (= a very important reason) beside each of these possibilities:

a ____ because of the place they are in.
b ____ because of what they are talking about.
c ____ because they don't know each other.
d ____ because of their education and personality.
e ____ other reasons _____

3 Are the following more likely to occur in formal or informal conversations?

a very polite expressions like 'Do you mind my ...'
b colloquial expressions like 'hang on', 'great', 'hey'.
c long complicated words like 'exquisite'.
d omission of subject, e.g. '(It's) Nice, isn't it'.
e special phrases to replace 'yes' and 'no', like 'certainly' and 'not at all'.

When people are speaking or writing, their choice of words is influenced partly by the meaning they want to get across, and partly by the situation they are in. It may be appropriate to use an **informal** *style (e.g. with close friends), a* **neutral** *style (e.g. with business acquaintances), or a* **formal** *style (for example, when writing a letter to a potential employer).*

ACTIVATE

4 With a partner, make up two short conversations, one formal and the other informal, in which one speaker apologizes to the other for spilling a drink on their clothes.

5 Look at the three letters. Which do you consider to be the most formal, which the most informal and which neutral?

a

Sir,
   The purpose of this letter is to express the dissatisfaction and frustration I have experienced at your hands over the last few years, and in particular in the course of the week just ended.
   As a regular passenger on the line between Effingham Junction and Waterloo, I have recently been among the sorriest victims of your unreliable and overpriced service. On at least three occasions during the last week, we have been kept waiting for periods of at least twenty minutes. On two other occasions, announcements were made to the effect that our usual services had been cancelled due to 'non-availability of staff'. . . .

b

Dear sir,

This is the fifth time that I've written to you to complain. I have been using the train service between Effingham Junction and Waterloo for three years now, and the trains are almost always dirty. They are also incredibly unreliable. This week, for example, three of my normal trains have been delayed for at least twenty minutes, and two have been cancelled altogether.

Please suggest ways in which British Rail could compensate me for the lost time and additional stress.

Yours faithfully,

c

Dear British Rail,

I have to say you really take the biscuit. Five times this week your bloody trains have left me standing on the platform for twenty minutes or more. Twice, the trains didn't even bother to appear.

Do you honestly think your passengers have got nothing better to do than stand around freezing to death? Maybe it doesn't matter if British Rail workers roll up to work half an hour late. I can tell you, though, that my boss won't stand for it. Enclosing a bill for lost earnings.

Please get your act together!

Yours,

List three reasons why you think one of the letters is *informal,* and three reasons why you think another is *formal.*

6 Which of these words and expressions from the letters is informal (I), formal (F) and neither formal nor informal (N)?

__ Dear Sir	__ the fifth time I've	__ the sorriest victims	__ just ended
__ twice	written	__ cancelled	__ overpriced
__ roll up to work	__ take the biscuit	__ please suggest	__ due to
__ regular	__ didn't even bother	__ bloody trains	
passenger	__ I can tell you	__ maybe	
__ to the effect that	__ at your hands	__ enclosing	

ACTIVATE

7 Which of the following things make you feel like complaining? Compare your answers with a partner's.

public transport
restaurants and public eating places
telephones
postal services
the police
television or radio
the health service
something else

Write a formal letter of complaint in English to one of these services.

8 With the help of a dictionary, try to complete this table:

Informal/colloquial	Neutral	Formal
_____	policeman	xxxxx
dough/dosh	_____	xxxxx
pad	_____	dwelling
boss	_____	xxxxx
xxxxx	_____	obtain

> As well as choosing more formal and informal words according to the situation they are in, people often use technical or specialized language to talk about a particular subject that they know about or are interested in. For example, when a doctor is talking to a nurse, he or she will use different words from when he or she is addressing a patient. Many other professions and activities, such as gardening, music, computing and engineering, have their own specialized vocabulary.

9 Do you use specialized vocabulary in your own language? If so, where do you use it and what subjects do you use it for? Discuss your answers with some other students.

10 Look at the following exchanges. Where would you expect to hear them, and who might the speakers be?

In a) and b), the special language is used instead of 'normal' language. Translate the exchanges into 'normal' non-specialized English.

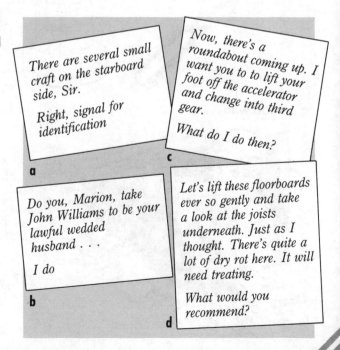

There are several small craft on the starboard side, Sir.

Right, signal for identification

a

Now, there's a roundabout coming up. I want you to to lift your foot off the accelerator and change into third gear.

What do I do then?

c

Do you, Marion, take John Williams to be your lawful wedded husband . . .

I do

b

Let's lift these floorboards ever so gently and take a look at the joists underneath. Just as I thought. There's quite a lot of dry rot here. It will need treating.

What would you recommend?

d

Often, as in dialogues **c)** and **d)** special language is used because the vocabulary is needed to refer to or describe technical things. Of course, many people don't know the technical vocabulary, and it is useful to be able to use other equivalent non-technical expressions.

ACTIVATE

11 Look at the pictures and complete the following descriptions.

12 Using a dictionary if necessary, find non-technical ways of saying the following:

a They're excavating the ruins.
b Mary's undergoing an appendectomy.
c Dissolve five grams of the powder in the acid and shake the solution.
d Before boarding, extinguish all smoking materials.
e Season lightly and simmer for five minutes.

a thing/tool for . . .   a machine for . . .   a vehicle for . . .

a person who . . .   a building in which . . .

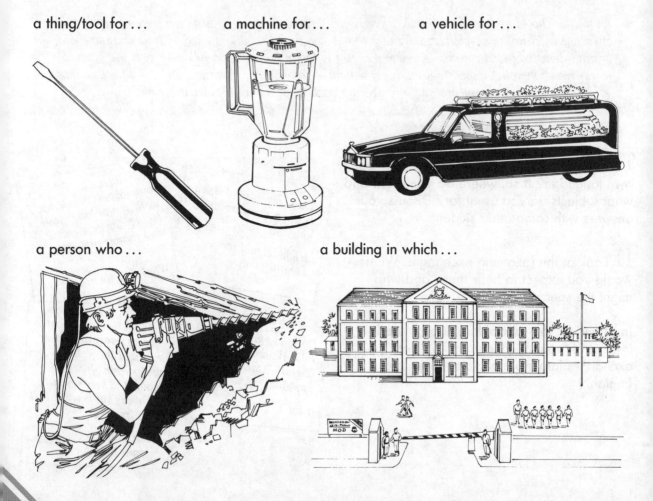

13 Look at the diagram below. Explain in
simple English how to put the table together.

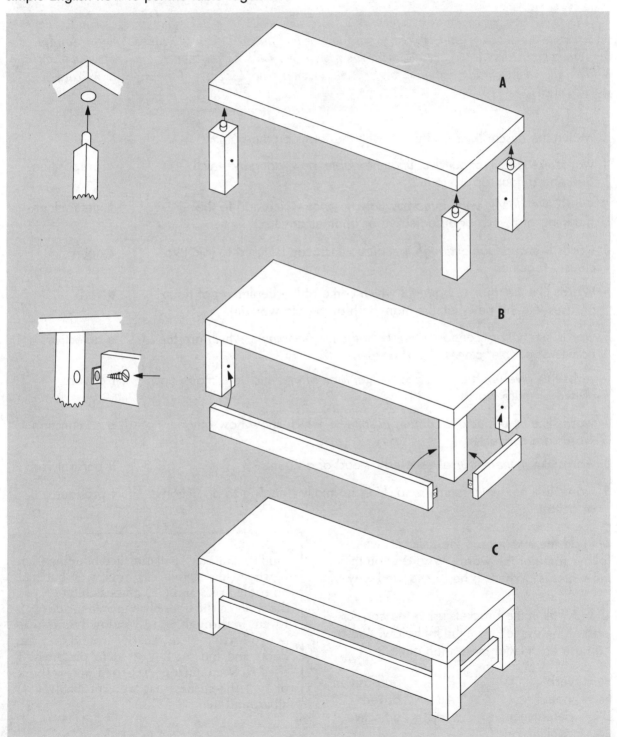

Parts of speech: verbs and nouns

*We know that by changing the form of a word we can change its grammatical meaning. For example the adjective **loud** can be reformed to give us **loudly** (adverb), **loudness** (noun), **louder**, **loudest**, etc. In order to 'know' a word you need to be aware of these changes and what they mean. To understand word formation it can be useful to know what the parts of speech (or 'word classes') are called.*

1 Match the descriptions on the left with the terms on the right.

1 words like *green, expensive, uncomfortable, new, naughty* which describe a noun or pronoun.   **a** preposition

2 words like *slowly, very, tomorrow, away, once* which add to the meaning of a verb or an adjective or another adverb.   **b** determiner

3 words like *and, but, although, because* which can be used to join two clauses together.   **c** noun

4 Words like *the, that, a, both, his* which come at the beginning of noun phrases (e.g. his new hat, the man, both of the old women).   **d** verb

5 words like *nation, London, school, footballer, happiness,* which are the names of people, places, things or ideas.   **e** adjective

6 verbs like *give up, run out of, look into, look after,* which are made up of two or more words.   **f** adverb

7 words like *in, off, next to, under, in spite of,* which show how other words are connected.   **g** conjunction

8 words like *it, them, ourselves,* used instead of a noun.   **h** phrasal verb

9 words like *be, walk, speak, read, hide,* normally referring to an action or a state.   **i** pronoun

2 Read the text. Ignore the brackets which follow some of the words. Who do you think the writer is? Where is he or she, and why?

3 Now fill in the brackets using the correct part of the speech from the list below. You can use each letter more than once.

V   =   verb
N   =   noun
D   =   determiner
C   =   conjunction

P   =   preposition
Adv =   adverb
Adj =   adjective

I hid ( ) in a ( ) half-finished building ( ). It was made of red ( ) brick ( ) but had no roof. Trees and ( ) grass as high ( ) as the walls of the house had grown inside ( ). I went in through ( ) a window frame so as not to leave ( ) any marks around ( ) the door, and hid fearfully ( ) in the grass. I tried to keep quiet ( ). I tried not to think of ( ) the snakes that were probably ( ) all around me.

*Verb endings signal changes in tense and aspect. There are two tenses, present and past. Present tenses usually refer to the present (but not always) and past tenses usually refer to the past (but not always). Aspect shows whether the verb tense (present or past) is **simple** (e.g. He walks, he walked), **continuous** (e.g. He is walking, he was walking) or **perfect** (e.g. He has walked, he has been walking).*

VERB ENDINGS

4 Complete this chart of verbs from the text.

Infinitive	Present participle	Past tense	Past participle
		hid	
	having		made
			grown
		went	
leave		tried	
keep			
think			

What is the difference between these verbs from the text and verbs like **talk, love, play** and **wait**?

PLURALS

Forming the plurals of most nouns is very straightforward. Others are more complicated.

5 Find the four plural nouns in the passage opposite. What is the singular form of each noun?

6 Work in pairs to find the plural of the following nouns.

a donkey
b tomato
c ox
d mouse
e mouse trap
f piano

g pheasant
h fish
i cloth
j syllabus
k ship
l star

m elephant
n man
o sky
p ostrich
q cello
r symphony

Check your answers in a dictionary. Were you right?

What do you know about the way we make nouns plural? Is one way more 'regular' than others?

7 Read the continuation of the story from page 28. You will find it on the next page.

a How accurate were your guesses in exercise 2?
b What other facts about the writer and his/ her situation do you know from this extract?

I waited.
I tried to make plans.
Instead I found myself thinking
of irrelevant things: cold beer, buttered
toast, the time one of my children had chicken pox.
I dozed. Hours must have passed, and there was a
rainstorm. It left me soaked again but at least, I
reasoned, it should have washed away most of my scent,
making it more difficult if they came after me with dogs.
I heard a helicopter overhead. I burrowed deep into the grass.
I didn't need a prize to guess that the helicopter was looking
for us. Later in the morning I heard gunshots. I was
relieved because they were a long way off. Then I was ashamed:
it meant one of the others had probably been shot. I felt sure it
must be Kasujja. He was the most vulnerable. Poor Kasujja.
They'd got him.
Then I saw movement in the grass. It was what I feared: a snake.
It was a mamba, very poisonous. I kept still, telling myself that
snakes attacked only moving
things, and then only because
they are afraid, not because they
are aggressive. I hoped the mamba
would remember this. It had seen me,
raised its head, lowered it again, and then raised it
once more, tongue flickering, as if preparing to strike.
I don't know how long this went on. It seemed like hours.
Then the mamba decided it didn't like the look of me,
executed a simultaneous turn, climbed a wall and was gone.

Wycliffe Kato *An Escape from Kampala* Granta
Volume 22 (Granta Publications)

8 Describe the place that the writer is in, and its surroundings. Make a drawing of it if that would help.

9 Discuss the following in pairs and/or groups:

a What reasons can you think of for hiding from somebody?
b Have you ever hidden from somebody (other than in a game)?
c What do you think of when you are miserable or frightened?
d How do you feel about snakes? What animals are you afraid of?

10 Invent an ending for the story.

ACTIVATE

11 Tell a story about hiding from something or somebody. The story should have two characteristics:

a It should use as many words as possible from the texts in exercises 2 & 7.
b It should be as unlike the story in exercises 2 & 7 as possible.

UNIT | 8 | *Affixes*

We often add things to the beginning or end of a word to change its meaning or grammatical status. We can make words have opposite meanings, (e.g. **happy – unhappy**) show that a verb is in the past (e.g. **wash – washed**) or make a noun into an adverb (e.g. **hope – hopefully**). How does this all work?

SUFFIXES AND PREFIXES

The ending of a word will often show what part of speech the word has become. For example the **-tion** at the end of **authorization** tells us that the word is likely to be a noun; the **-s** at the end of **hides** tells us that this is either the third person singular (present simple) of the verb **hide** or the plural of the noun **hide**.

1 In these words, taken from the text on pages 26 and 28, (see box) what endings are used for the following?

noun (singular)
noun (plural)
verb
adjective

2 Complete the table below. What endings:

a turn nouns into verbs?
b turn verbs and adjectives into nouns?
c turn nouns and verbs into adjectives?

> waited irrelevant children soaked
> ashamed vulnerable poisonous
> attacked aggressive flickering
> simultaneous movement

Think of other nouns, adjectives and adverbs. What other endings can you add to the list?

Noun	Adjective	Adverb	Verb
	quick		
simplification			
			legalize
dirt			
	painless		
		hopefully	
		xxxxx	drive
	stupid		xxxxx
		xxxxx	retire
		xxxxx	wash

PREFIXES (WORD BEGINNINGS)

*If word endings change the grammar of a word, word beginnings often change the meaning of a word. For example the word **irrelevant** in the text on page 30 means 'not relevant'. **Ir-** has the meaning of 'not'.*

3 What meaning does the first part of each of the following words have?

a **dis**approve	h **ex**pel
b **in**expensive	i **over**estimate
c **un**happy	j **pre**dict
d **il**legal	k **sub**tract
e **des**cend	l **co**incide
f **non**sense	m **re**arrange
g **im**possible	n **post**pone

Some of the words can be used without their prefixes (e.g. **a** *approve*) but some can't (e.g. **e** * *scend* is not possible). Which words are like **a** and which are like **e**?

4 Using beginnings (prefixes) make the opposite of the following words.

a kind
b literate
c temperate
d honest
e centralize
f regular
g resident
h polite

ACTIVATE

5 Complete the text with the correct form of the word in brackets. Check your answers in a dictionary.

The day that Carol ran away from school was one of great (1)_____ (anxious) for Miss Angela Beresford, the Headmistress. But then it had begun badly. She had woken up feeling very sick and (2)_____ (well) and at work almost all the teachers had been (3)_____ (agree) – not at all pleasant – because they were cross about the latest pay settlement. They had wanted a 10% increase, but she had only been able to offer them 5%. They started shouting at her and after a bit she (4)_____ (yell) back at them. Now she wished she hadn't. Even after ten years she still (5)_____ (estimate) the effect of her shouting. She didn't think that it would affect her teachers at all, but it always did. They would get very angry and as a result they would (6)_____ (active) work against her. The (7)_____ (discover) later that morning that Carol had run away (and run away, mind you, from the best upper-class girls' boarding school in the country) was quite (8)_____ (literal) the last straw. So when she found Carol's note – almost like a suicide's, completely (9)_____ (hysteria) – the thing that really upset her was the school's failure (and by (10)_____ (imply), hers) to teach Carol how to spell. 'i carnt stey here enimoor coz ov Miss Turner,' read the note, 'she is horibul.'

Angela Beresford read the note in
(11) _____ (amaze). The girl's (12) _____
(cruel) to Miss Turner was common knowledge. But it was then that she made the
(13) _____ (decide) to stop being a headmistress. Two weeks later she left the school
and joined the circus as a lion-tamer. It was
(14) _____ (considerable) more fun and
certainly less (15) _____ (danger) than her
previous job.

6 Why do you think Carol ran away? Did you
go to a boarding school? Would you send
your child to a boarding school? Why? Why
not?

SPELLING

7 Correct the spelling in Carol's note. Why do
you think she wrote the words in the way that
she did?

Spelling & sounds

English spelling is usually considered difficult. That is because there often appears to be no direct relationship between the way something sounds and the way it is written. Different spellings can have the same sound.

1 The following pairs of words have different spellings. Do they sound the same or different?

a flour   **b** ruff   **c** throw   **d** bow (down)
   flower   rough   through   bough

2 The following pairs of words have the same combination of vowels in their spelling. Is the sound of the vowels the same or different in each pair?

a thr*ough*   **c** sh*oe*   **e** k*ey*   **g** t*ea*m
   th*ough*   h*oe*   f*ey*   s*ea*nce
b c*ough*   **d** afr*ai*d   **f** s*ei*ze   **h** b*u*ry
   t*ou*gh   s*ai*d   r*ei*gn   b*u*n

SOME SPELLING RULES

Is there anything about English spelling which is regular, then? Are there any rules? How does spelling change when words have new endings?

3 Add *-ed, -d, -ing, -er, -r* or *-est* to the following words. Should you double the last consonant or not? Should you add a different consonant?

a hop	**f** fast	**k** excel	**p** picnic
b hope	**g** beat	**l** refer	**q** bat
c fat	**h** develop	**m** open	**r** marshall
d late	**i** begin	**n** visit	**s** omit
e phone	**j** rebel	**o** panic	**t** bleat

English has many spelling 'rules'. Can you work them out for yourself?

4 Using your answers to exercise 3, can you say what happens to the last consonant in a word when new endings are added in the following cases?

a the original word ends in one vowel + one consonant (e.g. *hop*).
b the original word ends in two vowels (or more) + one consonant (e.g. *beat*).
c the original word ends in one vowel + two consonants (e.g. *marshall*).
d the original word is a two-syllable word with the stress on the first syllable (e.g. *open*).
e the original word is a two-syllable with the stress on the second syllable (e.g. *refer*).
f the original word ends in a single l (e.g. *rebel*). (Note: this does not apply in American English.)
g the original word ends in a c (e.g. *picnic*).

5 Look at these words. What are the rules for a final *-e* when something is added to the end of a word?

a hope-hoping, rope-roping, fume-fuming, fame-famous
b see-seeing, agree-agreeing-agreeable
c knowledge-knowledgeable, orange-orangeade, replace-replaceable
d replace-replacement, hate-hateful, live-lively
e due-duly, argue-argument, true-truly

6 Look at the following words. Which are spelt correctly (c), which are spelt wrongly (w)?

a friend _____

b feild _____

c receive _____

d concieve _____

e believe _____

f ceiling _____

g seize _____

h greif _____

What sound is being spelt here by ei or ie? What is the rule? What has the letter c got to do with it? Why is seize an exception?

> *There are several differences between British spelling and American spelling; for example, in British English we write* **colour**, *while the Americans write* **color**.

7 Put A (= American English) or B (= British English) for each of the following spellings. Use a dictionary to help you.

a theater ( ) **g** theatre ( )

b humanize ( ) **h** refueling ( )

c humour ( ) **i** traveller ( )

d recognise ( ) **j** check (book) ( )

e colorless ( ) **k** sulfur ( )

f sulphur ( ) **l** cheque (book) ( )

ACTIVATE

8 Correct the spelling in the following children's sayings (collected by Nanette Newman in a book called *Lots of Love*).

I love my daddy becorse he give me a good ejukashun. *Zoe aged 6.*

My mummy sais I must love evreyboddy even the peple who killed my daddy but I dont. *Helen aged 7.*

My Dad went to prison and we have to keep remembring to love him. *Jean aged 7.*

My teecher is very crule. She smaks peple all days and she eats frogs legs and maks cros spells. I dont like her becose she says I tell fibs. *David aged 6.*

My father has à cros face in the holedays. *Joan aged 7.*

Old ladys arent reely old ladys. There just pepel waring old clothes. *Jamie aged 6.*

9 What do you think is the background to Helen and Jean's comments?

10 In groups decide on five adjectives to describe the following:
a a good mother
b a good father
c male children
d female children

|10| *Countable and uncountable*

1 Look at these exchanges:

A Would you like a ...?
  Yes, please.

B Can I offer you some ...?
  No, thanks.

Many different words could go in the empty spaces above. Look at the words listed below, and decide which words could go in which dialogue by marking them A or B. Then explain why. Do not change the words and phrases listed in any way.

__ milk	__ biscuit
__ medicine	__ brown sugar
__ new shirt	__ mineral water
__ day off	__ ride on my
__ chewing tobacco	motorbike
__ companionship	__ friendly advice
__ meal in a	__ useful information
restaurant	__ money
__ pair of scissors	__ help
__ banana	__ salt
__ ticket	__ work

*Nouns can be **countable** (like chair → four chairs) or uncountable (like **information**). It is important to know what kind of noun you are using because it may change the grammar of the whole sentence. For example, countable nouns may be singular or plural (e.g. **girl** → **girls, woman** → **women**); uncountable nouns are always singular (oxygen, but not *oxygens). Uncountable nouns cannot have **a** or **an** before them, and often have no article before them, (e.g.: I like coffee, Love is all you need.)*

Which of the words and expressions in the box above are countable, and which are uncountable?

2 Read the recipe on the opposite page. Is it something you would like to eat? Why? Why not?

List the underlined words from the ingredients in the two boxes below:

UNCOUNTABLE	COUNTABLE

Many words used to describe food and drink are uncountable. These can often be made countable by using words to indicate quantity.

3 For each of the quantities below, find at least one – and if possible three – appropriate kinds of uncountable food or drink.

a a slice of ...
b two spoonfuls of ...
c a loaf of ...
d a glass of ...
e a piece of ...
f a cup of ...
g three bowls of ...
h a bunch of ...
i a pinch of ...
j a drop of ...

Stir-fry Chicken and Vegetables
(for two)

Ingredients

boneless chicken <u>meat</u> *(200 grams)*	1 small <u>onion</u>
bean <u>sprouts</u> *(100 grams)*	1 clove of <u>garlic</u>
7 or 8 <u>mushrooms</u>	groundnut <u>oil</u> *(4 tablespoons)*
1 <u>green pepper</u>	soya <u>sauce</u> *(3 teaspoons)*
thin <u>noodles</u> *(100 grams)*	salt and <u>pepper</u> to taste

- Cut the chicken, pepper and mushrooms into small pieces. Chop the onion and garlic finely.

- Put 1 tablespoon of groundnut oil into the wok and heat well. Then add the chopped onion and garlic. Stir until lightly browned.

- Add a teaspoon of soya sauce and the pieces of chicken. Stir fry for eight minutes. Place the cooked chicken in a separate bowl.

- Put more groundnut oil in the wok. Then add the chopped pepper, with a teaspoon of soya sauce. Stir fry until tender. Add the chopped mushrooms. Stir fry for two minutes. Then remove from the heat.

- Boil a pan of water, and add some salt. Remove from the heat and place the noodles in the boiling water for three minutes. Then drain with a sieve.

- Put more groundnut oil and soy sauce in the wok and heat well. Then add the beansprouts. Stir fry for two minutes before adding the previously prepared noodles, mushrooms, pepper and chicken. Stir constantly for one minute, adding more salt, pepper and soya to taste. Then serve.

ACTIVATE

4 Write a short recipe in English for a dish that you like (and know how to prepare). Then join a group of three or four and exchange recipes. See if your dishes can be put together to make an interesting meal.

> *Remember that many words – e.g.* **coffee, beer, sugar** *– can be used both as uncountable nouns (e.g.* **I spilt some coffee on my trousers**) *or as countable nouns (e.g.* **Can I have two coffees please?**).

5 Tick (✓) the nouns in the following list which can have two different meanings, one when they are used as countable nouns (e.g. *Can we have three chocolate ice creams, please.* = separate servings of ice cream), and another related meaning when they are used as uncountable nouns (e.g. *You've got some ice cream on your shirt* = a drop or blob of ice cream). For each word that you tick, give two examples: one using it as a countable noun, and one using it as an uncountable noun (do not use *piece of, glass of*!).

> courage light wood homework
> mineral water cauliflower cola
> advice ice cream paper lamb
> parking salad information beauty
> anger weather hope smoking cake

Which words in the list above can only be used as uncountable nouns?

6 Which of the following is unusual or wrong? Why?

a Do you want a cola?
b I want some information, please.
c Could we have two teas and some cake, please.
d There is some apple on the table.
e David went to the baker's and bought three breads.
f She gave me some good advices.
g How much dollars do you have?
h Listen to the noises that animal is making. Strange, aren't they?
i What progresses have you made since we last met?

INVARIABLE NOUNS

> *A number of nouns can* **only** *be plural. This is often because the objects which they refer to consist of two equal parts joined together, e.g.* **trousers, spectacles,** *etc. In other cases it's just the way the English language has developed. Some plural nouns don't even have* **s** *at the end: e.g.* **police**

7 Which of these nouns *only* exists in a plural form?

> eyes binoculars feet shorts pyjamas
> clothes scissors earnings people socks
> premises cattle remains (eye)glasses
> thanks scales outskirts boots

A few other nouns that end in 's' can only be singular. The most famous is **news**. The others are names of some games, subjects at school or university, or diseases. Of course, these words must be followed by singular verb forms.

8 Look at this box which shows some common 'singular' nouns.

	games	*subjects*	*diseases*
news	dominoes	mathematics	measles
	billiards	linguistics	mumps
	draughts	classics	diabetes

ACTIVATE

9 Complete the following exchanges using the words in brackets to make correct sentences.

Example A: *I don't know what to wear to the interview.*

B: *(your green trousers/nice/why not/wear?)*
Your green trousers look nice. Why don't you wear them?

a A: Now, Ms Harper, how can you justify demanding a salary rise of ten per cent for your members?
B: (Because/earnings/dramatically affected by the rate of inflation)

b A: Hullo, Mrs Jones. You look very upset. What's the matter?
B: (Your cattle/in my garden/eat/my flowers and vegetables!)

c A: But, Doctor, I can't be that heavy!
B: (I can assure you/scales/checked and adjusted/only last week)

d A: Well, Jamie, back from school already? How was your day?
B: (OK/the good news/passed my English exam;/the bad news/was suspended for cheating)

e A: How did you know I was English?
B: (English people/usually/shy/and/other languages badly)

f A: I love playing pool.
B: (I think/billiards/much better game)

g A: Where do you work, Jack?
B: (My company's main premises/London, but I usually work/Manchester. The premises in London house/Head Office and Sales Department)

h A: Dad, can you give me a haircut, please.
B: (OK;/where/scissors?/I haven't seen/weeks)

10 Prepare a brief news broadcast for local radio or TV. It should contain three or four brief 'stories'. For example, a man is found sleep-walking to work, a member of the royal family tries unsuccessfully to cut the ribbon to open a new institution of some kind, or a house is raided by policemen at three o'clock in the morning after neighbours have complained about something.

Each story should involve using at least two words which always have the plural form. Begin: Here is the Local News . . .

TRANSITIVE AND INTRANSITIVE VERBS

1 Make up at least two appropriate endings for each of the sentences below. If possible, at least one of the endings should contain an object (for example, in *John drank some milk, some milk* is the object of *drank*).

_O_	a	The Prime Minister sent ...
___	b	The children played ...
___	c	The baby only sleeps ...
___	d	Can you help ... ?
___	e	Let's go ...
___	f	Put ...
___	g	Did you understand ... ?
___	h	Have you paid ... ?
___	i	Marilyn Monroe died ...
___	j	The rock star was wearing ...

Now, in the spaces on the left, mark the sentences O (= verb must have an object), NO (= verb can't have an object) or X (= verb can sometimes have an object, but can sometimes be used without). The first one is done for you.

*Many verbs can be used either **transitively** (with an object following – e.g. The children **ate the cake**) or **intransitively** (with no following object – e.g. The children **ate** at 2 o'clock). Some verbs are **intransitive** only. (e.g. The workmen **arrived three hours late**) (no object). Some verbs are **transitive** only. e.g. She lent her car to George (**her car** is the object).*

2 List below at least five other verbs which must be followed by a direct object and three verbs which can't be followed by a direct object.

Followed by a direct object (= transitive)	Not followed by a direct object (= intransitive)
put	sleep

3 The following letters were printed in a newspaper. Read them and find out:

a what the writer's problem is
b what attitude she seems to have towards her boyfriend
c why Jackie suggests she should say nothing

Dear Jackie,
I have a lovely boyfriend. Everything about him I love apart from one little thing. He is 1m 72 and should weigh about 65 kg. But he eats so much and takes so little exercise he is now 77 kg. He looks awful.
I try hard to encourage him, suggesting we play squash or go swimming together, but he says I'm always nagging him. I'm worried that although he's only 30, he's a prime candidate for a heart attack.
Anxious,
Southampton

Dear Anxious,
Perhaps you haven't got across to your boyfriend the fact that it's his health you're concerned about rather than his looks. If he thinks you're nagging him because of his appearance he will feel unloved and more in need of comforting food. But if he feels that, because you love him so much, you're concerned about losing him to an early heart attack, that could give him the impetus he needs to change his present unhealthy lifestyle.
Perhaps you should try by not mentioning his weight for a while. It may work wonders.

4 In a close relationship with someone of the opposite sex, which of the following would you find it hardest to tolerate? Put 1 beside the hardest and 5 or 6 beside the easiest to tolerate.

a _____ constant nagging
b _____ too much concern for your health
c _____ too much concern for your appearance
d _____ too much talking
e _____ laziness when it comes to household chores
f _____ other _____

5 As used in the letters, which of these verbs are not followed by objects?

love eats looks try nagging feel

ACTIVATE

6 Use these verbs (and others from the box above) in a brief dialogue between 'Anxious' and her boyfriend. Use the verbs in **bold** twice – once with an object and once without.

*eat weigh go die play **leave** get*

PHRASAL VERBS

7 Read the following poem quickly. What does it describe? Is it a happy or a sad poem? Why?

Single Mum

A penetrating cry:
She gets up, fighting off the sleep,
Puts on the old blue dressing gown
And switches on the blinding bedside lamp
For the third time that night.

'Come here':
She picks him up, the soft warm bundle,
And rocks in her arms the ruler of her life.
Mournful cries turn instantly to smiles
That say 'play with me tonight'.

It's three a.m.:
How can she turn him down?
How can she put him back?
There's space beside her in the wide wooden bed
For this bubbly baby and a cuddly toy or two –
Some comfort in the night.

8 Which of the following people do you think is in the most difficult situation?

a A single mother with the care of a young child or children.

b A single father with the care of a young child or children.

c A single parent with responsibility for teenage children.

d A single parent who only sees his/her child every two weeks.

e A child who hardly ever sees one of her/his parents.

f A child who lives with parents who often quarrel violently.

---

*Some verbs in English consist of two parts, e.g. **take up** (= begin to practise a hobby or sport). The first part is an ordinary verb, but the other part is a word like **up, on, across, off,** etc. Some of these verbs are called **phrasal** verbs. It is often difficult to understand what phrasal verbs mean at first because the original meaning of the verb and the **particle** (the other part) has changed, e.g. She **took over** the company means she **took control of the management** of it.*

---

9 Look at these phrasal verbs from the poem. What do they mean?

get up   switch on   put on   pick up
turn down   put back

---

10 What do the phrasal verbs in the following sentences mean?

a The plane *took off* more than an hour late.

b It was so hot Mary *took* her sweater *off/took off* her sweater.

c Roger didn't know what the word meant so he *looked* it *up* in the dictionary.

d *"Come on!* We're going to be late!"

e Claudia didn't want her old records so she *gave* them *away.*

f The Director *put* the meeting *off* until Friday.

g The car *broke down* so they had to walk home.

---

*Like ordinary verbs, phrasal verbs can be either **transitive** (followed by an object) or **intransitive** (not followed by an object).*

---

11 Which of the phrasal verbs in exercise 9 are transitive? What do you notice about the word order of these transitive phrasal verbs? Does the particle come before or after the object?

Complete the sentences in the box with *before* and *after.*

Sometimes the particle (on, up, down, away, etc.) comes _____ the object. Sometimes it comes _____ the object. It always comes _____ an object which is a pronoun (it, him, her). If the object is a noun, it can come _____ or _____.

ACTIVATE

12 Complete the following using phrasal verbs from the box and putting the objects of the phrasal verbs in the appropriate place.

If you are not sure of the meaning of a phrasal verb, use a dictionary.

> put up   bring up   invite out/take out
> ring up   split up   warm up   take back
> work out   send away   get up   set off
> pick up

Mike and Judy have two young children: Alison, aged 8 and Peter, aged 5. They are very lively and affectionate children, and both parents have enjoyed (1) _____ (them). But Mike and Judy's marriage wasn't (2) _____, and six months ago they decided to (3) _____.
Judy and the two children stayed in their small suburban house, and a friend from work (4) _____ (Mike) in his flat. Then Mike's company (5) _____ (him) to open a new office in the south of the country.
Now Mike only sees his children once a month, although he (6) _____ (them) once or twice a week. On the first Saturday of each month he (7) _____ on the 300 mile journey to the north.

He (8) _____ (the children) from their home about lunchtime and (9) _____ (them) to lunch at a hamburger restaurant. At first, father and children are almost like strangers, but then the conversation (10) _____, and they begin to talk about what they've been doing for the last month — life at school, their friends, their new toys. After playing in the park or seeing a film, it's time to (11) _____ (Alison and Peter) and leave them with their mother. The next day, Mike (12) _____ early, (13) _____ (the children) for lunch again, says goodbye to them with a heavy heart, and returns to the south. When he sees the expressions on his children's faces, he sometimes wonders whether his visits do more harm than good.

PREPOSITIONAL VERBS

There is another group of verbs with two parts. They consist of a main verb and a preposition (e.g. **look at, agree with**). *They are easier than phrasal verbs because their meaning is usually clearer, and because they always have an object which comes after the preposition, e.g.* **Mary looked at the picture, Mary looked at it** *(we cannot say* ∗*'she looked the picture at', or* ∗*'she looked it at').*

13 Which of the sentences on the right contain prepositional verbs? (You can test whether a verb is a prepositional verb by seeing whether it is possible to move the object next to the verb.)

a She broke off the relationship.
b He applied for a driving test.
c The board decided on a new plan for the company.
d John put on his sweater.
e The Director is relying on his managers.
f Who is looking after the children?

PHRASAL—PREPOSITIONAL VERBS

*Another small group of verbs has three parts, the last of which is a preposition, e.g. **How do you put up with the weather?**. These verbs are always transitive, and the object comes after all three words.*

14 What do you think the following mean?

a I'm not putting up with your tantrums any longer!

b These days you've got to stand up for yourself.

c Try to cut down on the amount of fat you eat.

d You must face up to your problems instead of trying to hide from them.

ACTIVATE

15 Correct any mistakes you find in these sentences. Then, with a partner, try to express the same meaning using different words.

a Put your clothes away. This room is a mess!

b Get the story on with: I want to know what happened.

c The plane took off three hours late.

d Bob: You made up that story, didn't you?
Sue: No, I didn't make up it.

e Can you put me up for the night? Hotels are so expensive.

f Get the car in. I'll drive you to the airport.

g Get the car out. I want to put my motorbike in the garage.

h John is going to stand in for Lynn while she's on holiday.

i Sarah: Where are my old jeans?
Dad: I've thrown away them.

j Get my bicycle off. I want to ride it now.

16 Imagine you work as a TV journalist. Use at least five of the following phrasal and prepositional verbs to prepare questions for an interview with a film or pop-star. Ask about his or her daily life, family, etc. Then ask a partner to play the part of the star and interview her or him!

PHRASAL VERBS: wake up, get up, put on, phone up, go out, take out, keep on (= continue), etc.

PREPOSITIONAL VERBS: agree with, believe in, belong to, listen to, look for (= search for), take after (= be similar to family member)

PHRASAL/PREPOSITIONAL VERBS: put up with, look forward to, face up to

Verb complementation

DIRECT AND INDIRECT OBJECTS

1 Here are some extracts from magazine advertisements. What do you think they are advertising?

Which of the ads sounds most interesting to you? Why?

CAMERA CENTRE

CHOOSE FROM OUR WIDE SELECTION OF TOP BRANDED CAMERAS AND ACCESSORIES OR FROM OUR DARKROOM EQUIPMENT, PAPERS & CHEMICALS
OPEN LATE TIL 7.30PM MON-FRI.

AGENTS FOR:-
MINOLTA
OLYMPUS
PENTAX
CANON
NIKON

OPEN EVERY DAY
DINN
GOOD HOMEM
EAL ALE, OPEN FIRE, BEER G
LARGE PARKING SPACE

Royal Oak
RESTAURANT

FRIDGE
AND
REEZER
EPAIRS

Leave us part of your estate and we'll build on it.

ELECTRICAL
REPAIRS
NO
CALL OUT
CHARGE

Usually just a couple of short treatments daily bring beneficial results. Which is why we're offering you a FREE 15 day trial.

To receive a brochure about our luxury cruises, simply send the coupon to Beth Chapman . . .

Phillips

• ELECTRIC SHOWERS
• GAS MULTI POINT SHOWERS
• THERMOSTATIC SHOWERS
• SHOW
• SHOW
• SHOW
ACCES
.... WE HAVE IT ALL!

ALPINE
BOARDING
KENNELS
TTERY

UALITY
MMODATION
TS & DOGS

BUILDERS
INDUSTRIAL & DOMESTIC

Each spoonful of warm, soothing Ticklex brings effective relief to all the family.

Every mum likes to give her family something a bit different.

plete Job
l Electrical,
bing &
fing Work.

INDOOR KENNELS * PERSONAL
SUPERVISION * SPECIAL DIETS CATERED
FOR * OPEN ALL YEAR ROUND
COLLECTION & DELIVERY
INDIVIDUALLY EXERCISED

SHOWERS
dial 100

INOCULATED
PETS ONLY

RK FULLY GUARANTEED

2 Each of the advertisements contains a verb which is followed by two objects. One is a person and the other is not. Sometimes there is a preposition **to** before the person. List the objects in the table opposite.

Verb	Personal object	Other object
e.g. offering brings leave give send	you	a free 15 day trial

Some verbs may be followed by more than one object, a **direct** object and an **indirect** object. In **She lent her husband the car**, **the car** is the direct object and **her husband** is the indirect object. Indirect objects relate to questions like: **Who did she lend it to? Who did she tell?** or **Who did she buy it for?**. Direct objects relate to questions like: **What did she lend? What did she tell him?** or **What did she buy?**

3 Read the following examples. All have prepositions before the personal 'indirect' object. Which do you think can be changed as in the example?

Verbs followed by a direct object + preposition + personal object

Example:
He lent some money to his daughter → He lent his daughter some money.

a They bought a drink for the bridegroom.
b We showed the photos to the police.
c We showed them to the police.
d David made the cake for his girlfriend.
e David made it for his girlfriend.
f I explained the accident to the police.
g The President said a few words to the children.
h The old man told a story to the visitors.

Now check the list opposite. Were you right?

Verbs followed by indirect object + direct object

POSSIBLE

He lent his daughter/her some money.
They bought the bridegroom a drink.
We showed the police the photos.
David made his girlfriend a cake.
The old man told the visitors a story.

NOT POSSIBLE

* We showed the police them.
* David made his girlfriend it.
* I explained the police the accident.
* The President said the children a few words.

4 Now choose the right completion for the following statements:

Many verbs can/cannot be followed by a direct object + preposition + personal object.

All/some/none of these can be used in sentences with the pattern: verb + indirect object + direct object.

It is/isn't necessary to learn which verbs can't take both patterns.

When the direct object is a short pronoun (e.g. it, him), the indirect object usually comes/ doesn't come before it.

5 In the following, put the indirect object and the direct object in the correct order. Use a preposition *only if necessary*.

Examples:

John gave (a present/Mary) → John gave Mary a present

Say (the magic words/him) → Say the magic words to him.

a George read (his children/a story) before they went to sleep.

b Could you buy (a loaf of bread/us) on your way home?

c Explain (us/your joke).

d I couldn't find (Susie/a clean pair of jeans).

e Didn't you promise (it/your mother in law)?

f The reporters asked (so many personal questions/the pop star) that she got angry in the end.

g Why didn't you mention (the pain/the doctor)?

h Return (me/the book) as soon as you possibly can.

i Why on earth did you lend (Justin/your motorbike)?

j It was embarassing: I had to borrow (£10/Ann).

ACTIVATE

6 Using at least three of the verbs in exercise 2, write three new advertisements or radio/TV commercials for products, companies, etc. that you like (e.g. for records/cassettes, clothes, a wildlife charity, fast food, etc.).

OTHER TYPES OF VERB COMPLEMENTATION

*Apart from indirect objects and direct objects, there are several other possible "complements" for verbs in English, and different categories of verbs are followed by different "patterns". For example, some verbs can be followed by another verb in the -ing form (e.g. **She enjoys skiing**), others by **to** + the infinitive of another verb (e.g. **He wants to leave**), and others by both (e.g. **They love swimming/to swim in the sea**). Another group of verbs can be followed by a direct object and then -ing or infinitive (e.g. **I saw you cross/crossing the street**).*

7 Look at the structures which come after the main verbs in these sentences:

a They heard the birds singing at 6 a.m.
b Her parents wondered why she had left home.
c The directors plan to open a new factory in Scotland.
d Try opening the tin with a screwdriver.
e The prison guards forced him to wash out the toilets.
f Did she mention that she was expecting a baby?
g George will cook the meal this evening.
h Mary made her son do the washing up.

8 Which of the formulae below describes each of the sentences in the passage?

a subject + auxiliary (e.g. can, will, may) + infinitive
b subject + verb + to-infinitive
c subject + verb + object + to-infinitive
d subject + verb + -ing form
e subject + verb + object + -ing form
f subject + verb + (that) + clause
g subject + verb (+ obj) + question word + clause
h subject + verb + infinitive (without *to*)

Now read this short passage. Match each of the numbered sentences in it to the sentence above with a similar structure.

Maria Suarez is a Peruvian doctor. She works in a town high up in the Andes. Many of the patients are Indian. (1)Luckily she can speak Quechua as well as Spanish. (2)She often listens to the local people discussing their problems and telling jokes. (3)Maria enjoys working in country areas. (4)But she thinks that the people living there need more financial help and opportunities for education.

(5)Later Maria wants to specialize in cardiology. However, that would mean returning to University in Lima. (6)Her husband, a specialist in agriculture, would prefer her to stay with him for at least another year. (7)Maria wonders whether she should insist on going anyway. (8)And would her husband let her live alone in Lima?

9 With a partner think of an example sentence for each of the verbs below to test which of the patterns above can follow them. There may be more than one. Then check your examples in a dictionary, and write a, b, c, etc. beside each verb.

> must begin finish like hope wonder
> make ask help see know

Remember: When learning new verbs, it is important to try to find out which structures can follow them. A good dictionary can help you do this.

ACTIVATE

10 Imagine you are writing a play about a modern couple living in a city in an English-speaking country. The woman, like Maria, has a career and wants to develop it by going back to college in another city. The man wants her to stay with him and start a family.

Prepare a dialogue between the couple in which they try to persuade each other of their points of view. Use at least six of the verbs above, with a variety of different structures. You can use the verbs in any order.

1 | *The human body*

MEANING

Part A   Unit 1

📖**1** Where can you find these parts of the body? Use a dictionary to help you put them in the appropriate places in the table.

> Adam's apple ankle
> armpit back big toe
> bottom breast calf
> cheek chest elbow
> eyebrow eyelid forearm
> forehead heel hip knee
> lip little finger little toe
> mouth navel nose
> nostril palm shin
> shoulder shoulder blades
> small of the . . . stomach
> thigh thumb tummy
> waist wrist

head	
neck	
arm	
hand	
upper torso	
lower torso	
leg	
foot	

2 Can you find the parts of the body in the illustration?

WORD USE

COLLOCATIONS
Part A   Unit 5

3 Do you know any more words for parts of the body?

4 Which of the following words can be combined with *-ache*?

> arm   leg   chest   back   elbow   tummy   bottom
> thigh   stomach   ankle   wrist   head

ACTIVATE

5 What is wrong with the people in the pictures? Where do they have an ache or a pain?

6 In groups choose one of the pictures.

a What is the reason for the person's ache or pain?
b What treatment would you recommend?

MEANING

Part A   Unit 1

7 What do the words in the box mean? Can you explain where they are in your body?

> bones   muscles   blood   lungs
> alimentary canal   kidneys   skin

8 Read the text opposite. What facts and figures can you find out about the parts of the body in exercise 7?

The human body is fantastic and it has many parts; there is a skeleton of 208 bones; more than 600 muscles which make up 35–45 per cent of the body's total weight; a blood system containing between 9 and 12 pints of blood, operated by a heart which during a lifetime does enough work to have lifted a ton weight 150 miles up into the air; a nervous system dominated by a brain which makes the biggest computer look like a child's toy; a pair of lungs which handle 500 cubic feet of air a day; a cooling system to stop us getting too hot which has between two and three million sweat glands; a feeding system which can handle about 50 tons of food in an average lifetime (not to mention a

25-foot-long alimentary canal); a reproductive system that has all too successfully populated today's world with more than 4,000 million human beings; an excretory system with kidneys capable of filtering 45 gallons of fluid a day; and 17 square feet of skin to cover everything and, as one doctor put it, 'to keep the blood in and the rain out.'

This is the body, an extraordinary piece of machinery that we have taken to the depths of the ocean and up to the moon. It is the animal which has invented language, art, science, sport, architecture, politics and religion. It has conquered the world and may yet destroy it.

Desmond Morris *Bodywatching* (Jonathan Cape)

9 Desmond Morris lists twelve parts (or systems) of the body. What are they?

10 Complete the following sentences with words and information from the text.

a The heart is incredible because _____.
b There are _____ in a human skeleton.
c The nervous system is dominated _____.
d The _____ filter liquid.
e The human body is covered _____.
f _____ weigh almost half of the total body weight.

WORD FORMATION

Part A Unit 7

11 Make adjectives from the following nouns.

Nouns	Adjectives
skeleton	
muscle	
blood	
brain	
skin	
sweat	

Do the adjectives mean the same as the nouns?

ACTIVATE

12 Tell a story about one of the following.
Use any *two* of the following verbs and as many words as you can from exercises 1, 4, 7 and 11.

> *notice   break   hit   hurt   admire   suffer*
> *touch   examine*

a Someone who went to the doctor and ended up in hospital by mistake.
b Someone who took too much exercise and who lived to regret it.
c A woman who was saved after being stranded in the jungle for four months.
d Someone who never wants to own a pet shark ever again.

WORD USE

METAPHOR
Part A   Unit 4

13 Write the correct word in each space to complete the idiomatic phrases.

> *head   heart   face   neck   stomach   foot   hand*
> *skin   arm   shoulders*

a 'Would you like to be a mountaineer?' 'Oh no, I don't have a very good _____ for heights.
b Don't get too involved with those people. Keep them at _____'s length.
c You may not like him, but you've got to _____ it to him. He's a financial genius.
d Every time he opens his mouth he puts his _____ in it. I've never seen anyone make so many embarrassing mistakes.
e She likes to keep her feelings to herself. She's not the sort to wear her _____ on her sleeve.
f I know I should go to the meeting but I just can't _____ it.
g I find horror films absolutely revolting and I just can't _____ them. They make me feel sick.
h The pass mark was 65% and he got 65.3%, so he made it by the _____ of his teeth.
i She will lose _____ if she has to admit she made a mistake.
j Ironing is my least favourite activity. It's a real pain in the _____.
k If I were you I'd vote for Joan Huddlestone. She's _____ and _____ above the rest.
l I hadn't the _____ to tell him I'd already eaten after he'd gone to so much trouble cooking dinner.

ACTIVATE

14 Choose at least three of the phrases from exercise 13. Say where and when they might be said and who they might describe. Use the phrases as part of a dialogue.

15 Choose a part of the body and write a description of the day from that part's point of view!

FOCUS WORDS
PARTS OF THE BODY

Adam's apple	chest	kidneys	shin
alimentary	elbow	knee	shoulder
canal	eyebrow	leg	shoulder blade
ankle	eyelid	lip	skeleton
arm	face (*n*)	little finger	skin
armpit	face (*v*)	little toe	small of the
back	finger	lung	back
big toe	foot	mouth	stomach
blood	forearm	muscle	sweat gland
bones	forehead	navel	thigh
bottom	hand	neck	thumb
brain	head	nerve	toe
breast	heart	nose	tummy
calf (calves)	heel	nostril	waist
cheek	hip	palm	wrist

FOCUS PHRASES

be a pain in the neck
be head and shoulders above
(have a) head for heights
by the skin of your teeth
keep somebody/something at
  arm's length

lose face
not have the heart to do
  something
put your foot in it
wear your heart on your
  sleeve

2 *Physical appearance and description*

1 Complete the following questionnaire in pairs. Then compare the results in groups.

HOW DO YOU RESPOND TO PHYSICAL APPEARANCE?

1 When you first meet someone, what do you look at first?

a their hair
b their face
c their eyes
d their mouth

e the front of their body
f the back of their body
g the clothes they are
  wearing
h other (please specify) _____

2 Which of the following will make you think most positively about someone? (Choose one only.)

a They are well-groomed.
b They are well-dressed.

c They have a good physique.
d They look interesting.

3 Think of two people that you find very attractive. What is the most physically attractive thing about them?

a _____   b _____

4 Think of two people whose appearance you find unusual or striking. What is the most unusual/striking thing about them?

a _____   b _____

5 Which of these people do you find most attractive? Why?

---

a

c

e

d

b

f

WORD USE

COLLOCATION
Part A   Unit 5

2 Which physical features do the following adjectives usually describe? Put them in as many columns as possible.

> weak   dark   thinning   pointed   curly   shiny
> wide   mean   receding   large   bright   protruding   strong
> generous   square   straight   wiry   appealing

Hair	Eyes	Nose	Mouth	Chin

ACTIVATE

3 Describe the people sitting next to you using the adjectives from exercise 2, and any other words or expressions you know.

WORD USE

METAPHOR
Part A   Unit 4

4 Look at the expressions *in italics*. Which of the emotions in the box on the right do they express?

a She's *as white as a sheet*.
b She went *bright red*.
c She *came out in goose pimples*.
d Her *eyes narrowed*.
e She was *wide-eyed*.
f She *pursed* her *lips*.
g She *gritted* her *teeth*.

> *disapproval*
> *shock*
> *wonder*
> *emotional excitement*
> *fear*
> *determination*
> *suspicion*
> *embarrassment*

Are there any equivalent idioms in your language which show how we represent emotions physically?

ACTIVATE

5 Tell a story which includes two of the idioms in exercise 4.

6 Read this introduction.

> In *Sour Sweet* by Timothy Mo, Chen and Lily,
> who are both Cantonese (from Hong Kong),
> live in London, where Chen is a waiter in a
> Chinese restaurant.

7 Read the text to find out:

a How Chen's appearance has changed.

b How he feels about Lily's appearance.

Working in the fields Chen had once had a physique which had been lean, tanned, and sinewy; now it was almost impossible to see the outlines of his ribs for the plump flesh which clothed them. Not that he was chubby, just prosperous, as he was careful to explain to Lily.

On Lily there were two opposing views. Chen did not think she was pretty. She had a long, thin, rather horsey face and a mouth that was too big for the rest of her features, and she smiled too frequently for a woman. She also had largish breasts and her hands and feet were a fraction too big to be wholly pleasing to her husband. It was her face, though, which really let her down (Chen had decided), being over-full of expression, particularly her bright black eyes which she had a habit of widening and narrowing when listening to something she found interesting. Probably there was too much character in her face, which perhaps explained the lack of Cantonese male interest better than any particular wrongness of an individual feature or their relationship to each other. Westerners found her attractive, though. Lily was unaware of this but Chen had noticed it with great surprise. That was if the second glances and turned heads on the street were anything to go by.

Timothy Mo *Sour Sweet* (Abacus)

MEANING

DICTIONARY DEFINITIONS
Book 2 Part A Unit 1

8 Find words in the text to match these dictionary definitions.

a healthily thin

b having muscles

c pleasantly fat, nicely rounded

d having little fat on the body, not fat

e pleasantly fat (esp. of children and young adults)

f an appearance that reminds one of a horse

9 In pairs discuss:

a What did westerners find attractive about Lily?
b What features of men or women are not attractive in your culture but attractive in another culture?

10 Describe Lily in a positive way.

MEANING

CONNOTATION
Part A   Unit 2

📖**11** Use a dictionary to say whether the following words usually have a *pleasant, neutral* or *unpleasant* meaning.

THINNESS

> *thin slim slender slight skinny emaciated underweight*

FATNESS

> *fat stout chubby flabby obese overweight plump*

📖**12** Use a dictionary to complete the male/female chart for these words:

a lean tanned sinewy muscular voluptuous well-built shapely
b good-looking handsome pretty attractive beautiful ugly hideous plain
c beard moustache glasses eyebrows

Male only	Female only	Male and/or female

ACTIVATE

13 Use words from this unit to describe the people in these photographs.

a in a positive way.
b in a negative way.

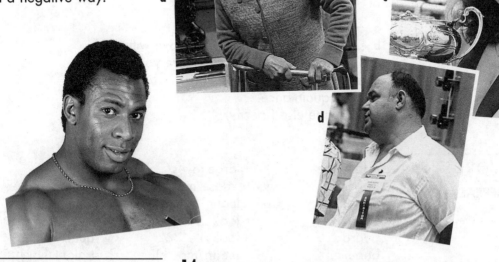

a

c

b

d

WORD GRAMMAR

VERB COMPLEMENTATION
Part A   Unit 12

14 What sentence patterns follow the verb phrases *in italics*? Choose the best answer **a**, **b** or **c**.

1 I *could tell* by his expression   **a)** to be   afraid.
           b) that he was
           c) as being

2 He *struck me*   **a)** as being   rather overweight.
           b) to be
           c) that he was

3 He *seemed*   **a)** that he was   very suspicious.
           b) to be
           c) being

4 He *appears*   **a)** to be   fairly relaxed.
           b) as being
           c) that he is

5 He *looked as if*   **a)** that he was   angry.
           b) he was
           c) to

6 He *looked*   **a)** to be   upset.
           b) being
           c) that he was

ACTIVATE

15 Write a description of either someone you know well and like a lot or someone you know well but don't like at all. Use words from this unit including *seems, appears, looks like, strikes me as,* etc.

Do not say who the person is. Other students read or listen to your description and they must guess if the person you describe is:

a a member of the family
b someone you are or were in love with
c your superior (in work or where you study)
d a child
e an acquaintance
f someone else (specify)

FOCUS WORDS
PHYSICAL APPEARANCE

appealing	large (eyes/	skinny
appear	nose/mouth)	slender
appearance	lean	slight
attractive	look as if	slim
beard	look like	square (chin)
beautiful	mean (mouth)	straight (hair)
bright (eyes)	moustache	strike one as if
chin	mouth	strong (mouth/chin)
chubby	nose	tanned
curly (hair)	obese	thin
dark (eyes/skin/hair)	overweight	thinning
emaciated	physique	ugly
eyebrows	plain	unattractive
eyes	plump	underweight
fat	pointed (nose/chin)	voluptuous
flabby	pretty	weak (chin)
generous (mouth)	protruding	well-built
glasses	receding	well-dressed
good-looking	seem	well-groomed
goose pimples	shapely	wide (eyes)
hair	shiny (hair)	wide-eyed
handsome	shining (eyes)	wiry
hideous	sinewy	

FOCUS PHRASES

be as white as a sheet	grit your teeth
(come out in) goose pimples	narrow your eyes
go red	purse your lips

WORD USE

COLLOCATION
Part A Unit 5

1 Which of the following words can be combined with *dressed* to describe the way people look in their clothes?

well   casually   nice   bad   badly   over   smartly attractive   untidy   untidily

Which of the expressions you have found is similar in meaning to the words below?

scruffy   elegant   dishevelled   relaxed

2 Look at these photos. Which of these words would you use to describe the way each person is dressed?

How would you describe the way you dress?

3 Read the following text and notice how the underlined words are used. Then complete the table below.

As it was his first meeting with Julie's parents, George thought quite hard about what he was going to <u>wear.</u> When going out with friends he normally <u>dressed</u> quite casually, but Sunday lunch with strangers was different.

Twelve o'clock — definitely time to <u>get dressed</u>. George put on a clean shirt and <u>tried on</u> the jeans he had bought the day before. They <u>fitted</u> him well, but they looked too new. He <u>took</u> them <u>off</u> and <u>put on</u> his dark green trousers. He would <u>wear</u> these and his leather jacket — and maybe a tie. But that didn't look right either — green just didn't <u>suit</u> him. Oh, God, why was he so vain . . . ? He <u>undressed</u> and started again.

	Transitive	Intrans.	Human subject	Inanimate subject
dress	✓	✓	✓	✗
fit	✓	✓	✗	✓
get dressed				
get undressed				
put on				
try on				
suit			✗	
take off		✗		
undress				
wear				

4 Complete the following sentences:

a Julie usually dresses . . .
b She got dressed . . .
c She put on . . . fitted . . .
d She wore . . .
e She tried on . . . didn't suit . . .
f She took off . . .
g She undressed . . .

5 Look at these pictures and at the clothes the people in them are wearing. Decide which clothes, in your opinion, are:

a the most attractive
b the most unusual
c the most comfortable and convenient
d the most formal

Discuss your choices with a partner.

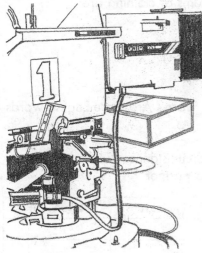

MEANING

6 Which of these items of clothing are being worn (or do you think are being worn) in the picture above? Put AR (actor), AS (actress), D (director) or C (cameraman) beside each item to indicate who is wearing them.

trousers	leather jacket	sweatshirt
T-shirt	shorts	pants
tie	dinner jacket	suit
vest	waistcoat	jeans
blouse	anorak	pyjamas
cardigan	overcoat	skirt
nightdress	boxer shorts	socks
bra	fur coat	bow tie
dress	tights	sari
leotard	tracksuit	shawl
boots	tennis shoes	shoes
sweater	knickers/panties	scarf
raincoat	dressing gown	stockings

7 Complete the following table to indicate how or when the items of clothing in the box in exercise 6 are normally worn.

on the top half of the body only:
on the bottom half of the body only:
on the top and the bottom halves of the body:
as underwear:
on the feet or legs:
in bed:
round the neck or on the head:
when the weather is cold:

In your country, which of these items of clothing are:

a usually only worn by women
b usually only worn by men
c worn only on informal occasions
d never worn by anyone

Which other items are commonly worn? Are there English words for them?

8 What would you wear in the circumstances outlined in the table? Discuss your choices with a partner.

	Weekday	Weekend
temp: 12 deg, cloudy		
temp: 25 deg, raining		
temp: 20 deg, sunny		
temp: −4 deg, snowing		
for an evening party		

WORD USE

METAPHOR
Part A Unit 4

9 Look at the expressions in *italics*. Match them with the phrases in the box below.

> *talking rubbish   don't get over-excited   be in charge
> smartest clothes   look gentler than you are   make an effort
> special smart clothes   get upset   very smartly dressed
> in the same situation*

a If I were *in your shoes*, I'd ask for a divorce.
b David used to beat me at tennis regularly, but *the boot's on the other foot* now.

c You're going to fail the exam if you don't *pull your socks up.*

d Hurry up, for God's sake. We're going to be late!
O.K., O.K. *Keep your shirt on.*

e Well, you know who *wears the trousers* in that household, don't you? It's certainly not Mr Thatcher.

f I know Clarissa's arguments are very persuasive, but I think she's *talking through her hat* myself.

g Don't be fooled by her friendly manner. She's *a wolf in sheep's clothing.*

h Why are you all *dressed up to the nines*?
Well, you said I should wear *my Sunday best*. Anyway, look at Mandy: she's *dressed to kill.*

i Oh, Fred, what on earth am I going to do?
Look, there's no need to *get your knickers in a twist*. Everything's going to be all right.

10 Read the passage. Where would you expect to read a text like this?

Fashion this autumn is going to echo the season — crisp, exhilarating and enjoyable. Whether you're shopping for a smart suit, a casual tracksuit or an outfit for a special occasion, you'll find the designers have given you a rich harvest to choose from.

Perhaps the only problem is what to choose when the weather doesn't quite behave as it should. Just what to do when summer clothes aren't quite right and it's too warm to swelter in a suit? Until now, the answer has been to opt for one or the other and hope for the best.

Jaeger has solved the problem in a way that other big names will undoubtedly follow. The company has combined the right styles with the right fabrics to see you through any occasion — and keep the temperature at just the right level. 'Keep colour in mind to maintain the spirit of summer, but look for lightweight wools and simple silhouettes for early autumn and to look good later as the weather cools,' advises Jaeger's Joan Jones.

It's a winning formula that shows to advantage in their simple but beautifully styled chemise dresses. The style comes in otter, emerald and violet in sizes 8–18.

(Bath Star)

11 Find words in the passage which mean:

a a suit of a kind worn by athletes, etc.
b informal
c items of clothing which can be worn together
d people who plan the way clothes will look
e fabric made from the hair of sheep
f materials for making clothes

12 Find words or phrases in the passage which tell you that the writer:

a likes autumn
b thinks there are plenty of good autumn clothes to choose from
c is comparing the climate to a human being
d thinks that there is a better solution to the problem of matching clothes to the climate this year
e thinks that the Jaeger solution is excellent

MEANING

SENSE RELATIONS
Part A   Unit 3

13 Can you find synonyms and opposites for the words in the table?

	Synonym	Opposite
stylish		
casual		
lightweight		
simple		
beautifully styled		
flattering		
alluring		

14 Complete the following exchanges with appropriate synonyms or opposites. Do *not* repeat a word that has already been used.

a A: Maria likes fashionable clothes, doesn't she?
B: Yes, she dresses in a very _____ way.

b C: Is this jacket suitable for formal occasions?
D: I think it's more appropriate for _____ wear, don't you?

c E: I was surprised how untidily dressed that applicant for the job was.

F: Yes, he was rather _____, wasn't he?

d G: You're looking terribly elegant this evening.

H: Thank you. My new suit is quite _____, isn't it.

e I: That's a very sexy dress Gloria's got on.

J: Yes, she thinks she looks _____. It doesn't leave much to the imagination, does it?

15 Discuss with a partner your ideas on the following subjects:

a your attitude to the fashions currently popular in your country and in other places in the world

b the influence fashion has on you when you choose clothes, and whether it is more important for you than price, style, comfort, colour, etc.

c the image of yourself that you try to convey through your clothes

d how clothes affect the way we react to other people. Are they important?

16 Describe your favourite clothes.

FOCUS WORDS

CLOTHING

alluring	knickers	stockings
anorak	leather jacket	style
blouse	leotard	stylish
boot	lightweight	suit (*n*)
bow tie	nightdress	suit (*v*)
boxer shorts	outfit	sweatshirt
bra	over-dressed	sweater
cardigan	overcoat	T-shirt
casual(ly)	pants	take off
designer	put on	tennis shoes
dinner jacket	pyjamas	tie
dishevelled	raincoat	tights
dress	sari	tracksuit
dressing gown	scarf	trousers
elegant	scruffy/scruffily	try on
fabric	sexy/sexily	underwear
fashion	shawl	undress
fashionable	shirt	untidy/untidily
fit	shoes	vest
flattering	shorts	waistcoat
fur coat	skirt	wear
get dressed	smart(ly)	well dressed
informal	socks	wool
jeans		

FOCUS PHRASES

be in somebody's shoes	pull your socks up
the boot's on the other foot	talk through your hat
dressed to kill	wear the trousers
dressed (up) to the nines	wolf in sheep's clothing
get your knickers in a twist	your Sunday best
keep your shirt on	

Health and exercise

1 Study the following pictures. For each one, decide where the person fits on the three scales 0–5.

unhealthy	0	1	2	3	4	5	healthy
unfit	0	1	2	3	4	5	fit
weak	0	1	2	3	4	5	strong

2 In pairs discuss where you think you fit on the scale:

a now
b in the past
c in the future

MEANING

IDIOM
Part A   Unit 4

3 Using a dictionary say what the phrases *in italics* mean:

a He's pretty *fit*.
b He's *a real picture of health*.
c I'm totally *out of condition*. I can't run another step.
d I'm *fighting fit*. I'll win.
e You seem to be *in* pretty *good shape*.
f She's *in* absolutely *peak condition*.
g Yes, I am rather *unfit*.

Which words helped you to come to your decision?

ACTIVATE

4 Use the phrases in exercise 3 to describe people you know or know about. Say why they are in the condition they are in.

Example   *My friend George is totally out of condition. But it's not surprising. He never takes exercise and he eats big lunches. His wife Clara is in absolutely peak condition, though. She goes to aerobics classes and plays a lot of tennis.*

WORD USE

COLLOCATIONS
Part A   Unit 5

5 Which of the nouns go with which of the verbs? Tick the correct boxes.

	Do	Play	Go
weight training			
golf			
aerobics			
badminton			
jogging			
yoga			
cycling			
rowing			

What other forms of exercise are talked about with the verbs *do, play* and *go*?

6 Where can you perform the activities in exercise 5? Put them in as many columns as possible.

gym	studio	track	court	course	outdoors

7 Read the two texts. Find the seven different types of exercise and say whether they are good for:

a aerobic fitness
b improving muscle tone

The 'four-limb' sports, such as rowing and cross-country skiing, seem to be especially good for the heart. 'When all four limbs are active, more blood is pushed back to the heart than when you are using just your arms or your legs,' says Dr Sharp. The muscles of the arms and legs use oxygen to produce energy – roughly five calories of energy for every litre of oxygen. This is how fitness experts are able to tell you that lying down, for example, you expend two calories of energy per minute, sitting three calories, walking four calories and running upwards of five calories of energy a minute.

It is not until you have been running for half an hour that you use up around 350 calories – which is roughly equivalent to the calorific content of a low calorie, pre-packed frozen dinner. 'If you want to lose weight you are better off performing a lower grade form of exercise such as walking or golf. You have a lower rate of energy expenditure but since you are doing it for so much longer the total number of calories used up is much more,' says Dr Sharp.

Jenny Bryan *Observer* magazine

You need a lot of self-discipline to use a home-based gym properly: pumping iron can improve your body but not without determination and sweat.

Home gyms consist of a stack of iron weights on two parallel vertical runners, with a padded bench attached at right angles. The idea is that you sit or lie on the bench and, using the various attachments, push and pull the weights with your arms and legs.

Weight training will improve muscle tone but it does not produce aerobic fitness and stamina, which you have to achieve by jogging or cycling. A home gym and an exercise bicycle is the ideal combination: the bike also helps you warm up before your workout.

Peter Knight *Expression* magazine

MEANING IN CONTEXT

8 What do the following words and phrases from the text mean?

> a 30-minute run   work out   four-limb sports
> lose weight   pumping iron   aerobic stamina
> calorie   warm-up   energy

Use them in the following sentences together with information from the texts. (You may have to change their form.)

a _____ are especially good for the heart.

b Oxygen produces _____ which is measured _____.

c The calorific content of a pre-packed frozen dinner _____.

d It is always good to do a _____ activity before _____.

e Weight training (sometimes referred to as _____) does not _____.

MEANING

9 Match the type of exercise with the pictures.

> skipping   squat jumps
> touching (your) toes
> sit up   press-up

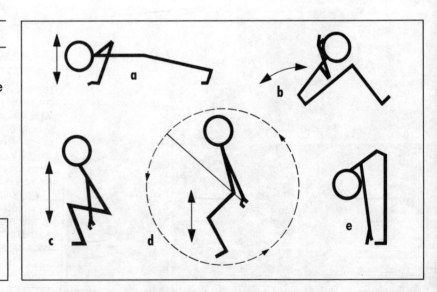

10 Give instructions to other students about how they should do one of the exercises.

Example *Lie on your back with your legs straight out in front of you ...*

ACTIVATE

11 Look at the pictures. Say what the people are doing and what benefits they are likely to achieve with these forms of exercise.

WORD GRAMMAR

PHRASAL VERBS
Part A   Unit 11

12 Put the correct preposition(s) in the blanks.

a You ought to cut _____ _____ cakes and biscuits for a start!
b If I were you I'd go _____ a diet.
c You're putting _____ too much weight.
d You should take _____ a new sport – like tennis or golf.
e You should be _____ a strict diet.

ACTIVATE

13 Write a dialogue in which someone who is unfit, overweight or feeling generally run down asks a friend for advice. Use phrasal verbs from exercise 12 and other words from this unit.

WORD USE

METAPHOR
Part A   Unit 4

14 Which of the people are talking about:

a someone who is morbid
b an architectural plan
c a politician
d children who watch television
e a prospective employee
f a sick child

15 Fill in the blanks with words from exercise 14.

a He's not _____ to be seen in public.
b They have a very _____ attitude to the problem. They don't seem to realize the damage that kind of thinking will do.
c He has a _____ disregard for pompous people — people who think they are superior when in fact they are not.
d You need a lot of _____ for this job.
e Your cat looks in pretty good _____. You've obviously been looking after it.
f If you live on a daily _____ of bad news you are bound to become disillusioned.

ACTIVATE

16 Design an advertisement for a newspaper about one of the following:

a A new rowing machine for home fitness exercises.
b An aerobics class.
c A sports club.
d A new exercise plan for the successful business executive.

Say what the activity/place, etc. actually does.

FOCUS WORDS
HEALTH AND EXERCISE

aerobics	golf (course)	skip
aerobic (fitness/ stamina)	gym	squat jump
	healthy	stamina
badminton (court)	heart	strong
calorie	jogging	sweat
condition	lose weight	take up (a sport)
cut down on	muscle	touch (your) toes
cycle (track)	muscle tone	unfit
cycling	overweight	unhealthy
(go on a) diet	oxygen	walk
energy	press-ups	warm-up
(take) exercise	pump iron	weak
exercise bicycle	put on (weight)	weight training
fit	rowing	work-out (*n*)
fitness	run	work out (*v*)
four-limb sport	sit-up	yoga

FOCUS PHRASES

be a picture of health	(have a) healthy attitude/ disregard
be fighting fit	(have an) unhealthy attitude/ fascination
be in good shape	
be in peak condition	
be out of condition	

Sickness and cure

WORD USE

COLLOCATIONS
Part A   Unit 5

1 Which words from column A go with words from column B?

Example *broken ankle, sprained angle,* but not *sprained leg

A		B	
sprained		leg	
broken		ankle	
twisted		arm	
fractured		wrist	
pulled		skull	
torn		shoulder	
black		ligament	
dislocated		muscle	
swollen		eye	
bruised		toe	
		finger	

ACTIVATE

2 In groups describe to other members of the group one of the injuries mentioned in exercise 1 that you have suffered.

a How did it happen?
b How was it treated?

MEANING

Part A   Unit 1

3 Match the words with the pictures.

dentist   doctor   nurse
optician   psychiatrist
surgeon

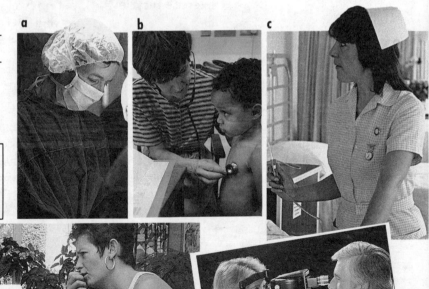

📖**4** Using a dictionary, make sure that you know the meaning of the following:

a an injection
b a sick note (for your employer)
c a blood test
d an eye test
e a prescription
f a filling
g an operation
h electric shock therapy

Who (from exercise 3) might administer these things?

5 Which of the people in exercise 3 would you prefer to marry? Why?

MEANING

SENSE RELATIONS
Part A   Unit 3

📖**6** What is the difference in meaning between the following pairs of words? (Use a dictionary to help you.)

a i) I've been *sick*.
   ii) I've been *ill*.
b i) Ow. I've *hurt* my hand.
   ii) I've *injured* my hand.
c i) Six people were *wounded*.
   ii) Six people were *injured*.
d i) My hand is *itching*.
   ii) My hand is *hurting*.

7 Complete the following sentences with one of the words from exercise 6. (Be prepared to use different forms of the words.)

a If you eat all that chocolate you'll make yourself _____.
b 'Stop scratching your mosquito bites.' 'I can't help it, they're really _____.'
c He was _____ on the first day of the battle and this, ironically, saved him from almost certain death.
d She's been _____ for almost three weeks and the doctors still can't tell what's the matter with her.
e My leg is _____ so much that I can't put my weight on it.

8 Read this passage from a romantic novel, *The Keeper of Innismullen*. What is the reason for the situation?

Their ill-fated marriage started badly on the first night, for when they arrived at the hotel and had unpacked their things Charles found that he was unable to hide his unhappiness. Despite his apologies, and his claims that he had not meant to hurt her feelings, Matilda's pride was deeply wounded and since she was unable to guess at the cause of his distress she jumped to all sorts of conclusions.

Charles was, by this time, ill at ease, but had no way of explaining the true situation to his new bride. Sick at heart, he continued to give unconvincing apologies or merely to murmur in monosyllables.

Finally, after three hours, during which Matilda's injured pride pained her more with every passing second, she exploded.

'I am sick and tired of this ill-mannered behaviour,' she exclaimed. 'I consider our marriage to be already at an end.'

She spoke in anger; how could she know that it would be five long years before her wish finally came true?

WORD USE

METAPHOR
Part A   Unit 4

ACTIVATE

📖**9** How are the words *sick, ill, injured, wounded* and *hurt* used in the extract from *The Keeper of Innismullen*? What other meanings can you find for these words in the dictionary?

10 Read this summary of the first part of a story called *Runaway Heart*.

Gregorio and Sylvia are terribly in love and hope to get married. Gregorio is invited to a dinner party to meet Sylvia's family, but her lover and her father have a terrible argument and Gregorio is thrown out of the house and told never to return. What are Gregorio and Sylvia to do now?

Tell the story in your own words, trying to use as many expressions from the text in exercise 8 as possible.

11 Put the following conversation between a doctor and a patient in the correct order (the first one has been done for you).

[1] Good morning.

[ ] Hello, Doctor.

[ ] Well doctor, I'm not feeling very well. I've got these awful pains in my stomach and I haven't been sleeping at all well.

[ ] Yes. Now I'm going to give you these pills. I want you to take two pills three times a day.

[ ] Well yes, I have had a bit of a high temperature, actually.

[ ] Oh have I, Doctor?

[ ] Mmm. It looks to me as if you've got some kind of a stomach infection.

[ ] Thank you, Doctor, thank you.

[ ] Now then, how can I help you?

[ ] Do you have any other symptoms? A temperature, for example?

MEANING

Part A   Unit 1

📖**12** What do the words and expressions *in italics* mean? (Use a dictionary to help you.)

a What are your *symptoms*?
b I'm not *feeling very well.*
c I'm *feeling rather low/under the weather.*
d I've got a *sore throat.*
e I've got *pains in my chest.*
f You've got a *(high) temperature.*
g You've got an *infection.*
h Take these *pills.*
i Get *plenty of rest.*

ACTIVATE

13 In pairs invent conversations in which a patient goes to visit their doctor.

14 The following scenes are from the TV soap opera *Hospital of Love*. Complete the blanks with the following words.

> operation   injection
> pull through   condition
> nurse   bear   took out
> hurting

SCENE IX
Doctor Martin Mills is at the side of Marcia Jaramillo's bed.

MILLS: Are you in any discomfort?
JARAMILLO: Yes, yes, Doctor, my leg is a)_____ terribly.
MILLS: Well then, I think I'll give you a painkilling
                 b)_____. And I'll make sure c)_____ gives you
                 something to help you sleep.
JARAMILLO: Doctor?
MILLS: Yes, Marcia?
JARAMILLO: Couldn't you stay with me, just for a bit? The pain
                 would be, somehow, easier to d)_____.
MILLS: But Marcia, I do have other patients to see.
JARAMILLO: Oh Doctor . . .
The camera fades out on a close up of Marcia's pleading face.

SCENE X

Mrs Jackson is talking to the surgeon, Katie Griffiths. Behind the doctor, through the window, we can see Mr Jackson in the recovery room tied to tubes, etc. With Mrs Jackson there is a tall good-looking man who is considerably younger than she is.

GRIFFITHS: Well, Mrs Jackson, the e)_____ went well. We
                 f)_____ your husband's appendix. We were only
                 just in time.
JACKSON: Oh! Is he going to be all right?
GRIFFITHS: That's difficult to say. Right now he's in a stable
                 g)_____ and I think he'll h)_____.
JACKSON: You mean . . . you think he's going to make it?
GRIFFITHS: Yes, I do. But you don't seem to be as pleased as I
                 expected.

JACKSON:	Oh yes, of course I am, aren't I, James?
GRIFFITHS:	James?
JAMES:	Oh yes, Doctor. I'm Mrs Jackson's friend. I've come to help her through this difficult time.
GRIFFITHS:	How very thoughtful of you!

The camera pans away towards the reception desk for Scene XI.

ACTIVATE

15 Write one of the following three scenes from *Hospital of Love*. Use as many words as possible from exercises 8, 12 and 14.

a Doctor Griffiths has to tell Mr Green that his wife is going to have quintuplets.

b The nurse has to tell handsome pop star Ricky Watts that he is going to have an operation.

c Doctor Mills, who is feeling ill, is talking to a female colleague who is secretly in love with him.

FOCUS WORDS
SICKNESS AND CURE

appendix	hurt (v)	pull through
black eye	ill	recovery
blood test	ill-fated	sick
broken (arm/leg)	ill-mannered	sick note
bruised	infection	sore throat
cold (n)	injection	sprained (ankle/
(stable/critical)	injure	wrist)
condition	nurse	surgeon
dentist	operation	swollen (leg/finger)
dislocated (shoulder)	optician	symptom
doctor	pain(s)	take out
electric shock therapy	patient	temperature
eye test	pill	torn (ligament)
feel (low/under the	prescription	twisted (ankle)
weather/well)	psychiatrist	virus
filling	pulled (muscle/	wounded
fractured (skull)	ligament)	wounded (pride)

FOCUS PHRASES

be sick and tired of	hurt somebody's feelings
be sick at heart	be ill at ease
be under the weather	

Ages and ageing

1 Think of two adjectives to describe:

a your grandmother
b grandmothers in general

Compare your words with your neighbour's.

2 Read the text and choose an adjective to describe:

a George
b George's grandmother

'You know what's the matter with you?' the old woman said, staring at George over the rim of the teacup with those bright wicked little eyes. 'You're *growing* too fast. Boys who grow too fast become stupid and lazy.'

'But I can't help it if I'm growing fast, Grandma,' George said.

'Of course you can,' she snapped. 'Growing's a nasty childish habit.'

'But we *have* to grow, Grandma. If we didn't grow, we'd never be grown-ups.'

'Rubbish, boy, rubbish,' she said. 'Look at me. Am I growing? Certainly not.'

'But you did once, Grandma.'

'Only *very little*,' the old woman answered. 'I gave up growing when I was extremely small, along with all the other nasty childish habits like laziness and disobedience and greed and sloppiness and untidiness and stupidity. You haven't given up any of these things, have you?'

'I'm still only a little boy, Grandma.'

'You're eight years old,' she snorted. 'That's old enough to know better. If you don't stop growing soon, it'll be too late.'

'Too late for what, Grandma?'

'It's ridiculous,' she went on. 'You're nearly as tall as me already.'

George took a good look at Grandma. She certainly was a *very tiny* person. Her legs were so short she had to have a footstool to put her feet on, and her head only came half-way up the back of the armchair.

'Daddy says it's fine for a man to be tall,' George said.

'Don't listen to your daddy,' Grandma said. 'Listen to me.'

'But how do I stop myself growing?' George asked her.

'Eat less chocolate,' Grandma said.

'Does chocolate make you grow?'

'It makes you grow the *wrong way*,' she snapped. 'Up instead of down.'

Grandma sipped some tea but never took her eyes from the little boy who stood before her. 'Never grow up,' she said. 'Always down.'

'Yes, Grandma.'

'And stop eating chocolate. Eat cabbage instead.'

'Cabbage! Oh no, I don't like cabbage,' George said.

'It's not what you like or don't like,' Grandma snapped. 'It's what's good for you that counts. From now on, you must eat cabbage three times a day. Mountains of cabbage! And if it's got caterpillars in it, so much the better!'

Roald Dahl *George's Marvellous Medicine* (Puffin books)

3 Find words or phrases which mean:

a to develop from being a child to being a man or woman
b (*derogatory*) immature, like a child
c (used especially by and to children) a fully grown person
d (idiom) you shouldn't behave as you do considering your age

4 Give a visual description of Grandma.

5 The extract comes from a book for children.

a Did you read books like this when you were a child?
b Would you like to have read this as a child? Why?

MEANING

Part A   Unit 1

6 Look at the examples and then copy and complete the chart using the words below. Use a dictionary to help you. Do any of the words refer to only males (M) or only females (F)?

> *young   juvenile   adolescent   teenager   mature*
> *grown-up   veteran   retired   elderly   senile   ancient*
> *baby   man   boy   lady   girl   toddler   kid*
> *youngster   senior citizen   OAP*

infancy . . . childhood . . . youth . . . adulthood . . . middle-age . . . old age

├Child────┤

├──lad (M)──┤

├── Woman (F) ──────┤

WORD FORMATION

PARTS OF SPEECH
Part A   Unit 7

7 Use a dictionary to complete the chart as far as possible. Notice, for example, that there is no noun to describe a mature person. We have to use the adjective + noun combination (*mature person/woman*, etc.).

State (noun)	State (adjective)	Person (noun)
adolescence		
	retired	
maturity		
		infant
		woman
manhood		
	youthful	
childhood		

ACTIVATE

8 In the following dialogues, agree forcefully with the first speaker. Use words from exercises 6 & 7 that mean roughly the same as the word *in italics*.

a Isn't she very *old*?
  – Yes. She's absolutely _____.
b I think he's a *child*.
  – Yes, he's just a _____.
c He's really *immature*, isn't he?
  – Yes, he is rather _____.

Now disagree forcefully with the first speaker. Use words from exercises 6 & 7 that mean roughly the opposite of the words *in italics*.

d You're just a *youngster*.
  – No I'm not. I'm quite _____.
e He seems very *childish* to me.
  – Oh really. I think he's rather _____ for his age.
f You're really *middle-aged*.
  – I don't agree. I've always thought of myself as _____.

9 What ages do you associate with the following characteristics?

> *wisdom   exuberance   creativity   attractiveness*

Find the opposite of the characteristics and say what ages you associate with them.

WORD USE

STYLE AND REGISTER
Part A   Unit 6

10 What do the following expressions mean if the speaker is:

— 20?
— 40?
— 60?

a He's *getting on a bit*.
b She's *pushing 40*.
c He's *no spring chicken*.
d She's *in her prime*.
e He's well *past his 'sell-by' date*.
f He's a bit *past it*.
g She's got *one foot in the grave*.
h She's just a *babe in arms*.
i He's rather *young for his age*.
j He's *over the hill*.

Do you think these expressions are neutral, formal or informal?

WORD USE

COLLOCATIONS
Part A   Unit 5

11 Choose the most appropriate adjective to complete the following sentences:

a The level of _____ crime is beginning to worry police.
   a) childish b) immature c) juvenile

b Joan would be a good candidate. She is a _____ campaigner.
   a) seasoned b) grown-up c) old-aged

c One of the features of this property is the number of _____ trees.
   a) seasoned b) mature c) veteran

d There is a London to Brighton rally of _____ cars every year.
   a) seasoned b) mature c) veteran

e Why don't you _____, you silly boy!
   a) come of age b) mature c) grow up

f Don't worry about his loud behaviour. It's just _____ exuberance.
   a) childish b) immature c) youthful

WORD USE

CONNOTATIONS
Part A Unit 2

12 Say which of the following words have *neutral, pleasant* or *unpleasant* connotations.

a young
b childish
c immature
d youthful
e grown-up

f adult
g mature
h old
i senile

ACTIVATE

13 Using words and phrases from this unit, write a dialogue in which two people are criticising an acquaintance of theirs.

14 Read these poems. Are they concerned with the same theme or different themes?

> ### Old Friend Seen on TV
>
> *Stania*
> *what's happened?*
> *A practical joke.*
> *They've put a bag on your head*
> *painted an old man's face on*
> *stuck a wig on top.*
> *You'll take it off*
> *won't you?*
> *You'll roar with laughter*
> *drink beer*
> *and tell us all your plans.*
> *Stania*
> *won't you?*
>
> Michael Swan

> ### Piano Piece
>
> A man bought a piano for his wife
> which she constantly tunes
> and polishes. He says her hands and fingers
> are less flexible than once they were
> which is depressing.
>
> She came home and she found it there,
> a big surprise. Its brown respectability
> dominates the room. He watches her straight back
> and fumbling fingers in the evening city, lit
> by brakes and klaxons.
>
> Peter Hedley

15 In groups decide on a word which expresses the mood of each poem.

16 In groups discuss the following.

Which three things do you most look forward to about old age?
Which three things do you least look forward to about old age?

ACTIVATE

17 Write a short composition about what has been, is or will be the best age for you and why.

FOCUS WORDS

AGE AND AGEING

adolescent	grow (*v*)	man	senior citizen
adult	grown up (*v*)	manhood	teenager
adulthood	grown-up (*n*)/(*a*)	mature	toddler
ancient	immature	middle age	veteran
baby	infancy	middle-aged	woman
boy	infant	old	womanhood
child	junior	old age	young
childhood	juvenile	OAP	youngster
childish	kid	retired	youth
elderly	lady	seasoned	youthful
girl	maiden	senile	

FOCUS PHRASES

babe-in-arms	no spring chicken
be getting on a bit	old enough to know better
be pushing (40, 60, 70)	past it
come of age	past your sell-by date
have one foot in the grave	young/old for your age
in his/her prime	

Birth and death

WORD USE

1 Look at the following announcements. What are they announcing?

> **Houghton** On September 6th at St Mary's Paddington to Mark and Angela (nee Jones) a boy, Timothy John

> **Robertson** On 12th October, peacefully at home, George, beloved husband of Kate and father of Ben & Emily. Private funeral. No flowers please. Donations to Cancer Research Campaign.

What do you know about the following people and places?

a St Mary's
b Mark
c Jones

d George
e Kate
f Ben & Emily

2 Is there any difference between these announcements and the way similar events are announced in your country?

3 What do relatives and friends do when a baby is born in your culture?

MEANING

Part A   Unit 1

4 Check the meaning of the words in italics. Put the mixed-up lines of the poem in the correct order. The first line has been identified for you.

SALLY'S EXCUSE FOR WATCHING TOO MUCH TV

> 1 You are *conceived*

> Not much of a story,

> You are *born*

> You *die*

> You get *pregnant*

> Is it?

> You *give birth*

What is the mood of the poem? Do you agree with it?

MEANING

Part A   Unit 1

📖**5** Look up the meaning of any of the words in the box you do not understand. Now put them in the correct places in the passage below (you may have to change the form of the words).

> *labour   birth   born   caesarean   contractions   expect*
> *give   become*

Mary first (1)_____ pregnant at the age of twenty-three. When she realized she was (2)_____ both she and her husband were very happy. It meant that they would finally start the family they had been looking forward to.

Mary was in the middle of writing an article for the local paper when she felt the first (3)_____. She phoned Steve and he rushed home in order to take her to hospital for he was going to be present at the (4)_____.

It was a long (5)_____ and in the end things got a bit difficult so the doctors had to give Mary an emergency (6)_____. At this point Steve fainted. But everything else went well and the baby was (7)_____ at exactly six o'clock in the morning.

Mary has (8)_____ birth to six more children since then – and each time Steve has fainted. Now they both think it's time to stop. She's fed up with giving birth and he's had enough of bumping his head on the hospital floor!

WORD FORMATION

Part A   Unit 8

📖**6** Add the words in the box to the stem 'birth'. Do you get one word or two ?

birth +

| control |
| mark |
| rate |
| place |
| right |

What do the new words mean? What other words do you know which are made up of two different words?

7 How many babies are there if you have:

a quintuplets
b triplets
c sextuplets
d quadruplets
e twins

What are identical twins?

ACTIVATE

8 In pairs tell each other everything you know about:
either a your own birth (where you were born, when, what everybody did, etc.).
or b the birth of a relative or friend's baby.

WORD USE

METAPHOR AND
EUPHEMISM
Part A   Unit 4

9 Look at the following expressions. Which of them mean

a die
b a dead person
c dead

pass on   the late Sheelagh Graham   pass away
kick the bucket   give up the ghost   at peace   the deceased

Do you have euphemisms like these in your language? Can you translate them into English?

WORD USE

COLLOCATIONS
Part A   Unit 5

10 In these commonly used phrases about dying, put the correct preposition or adverb in each space.

a She *died* _____ *natural causes.*

b After his wife's death he just seemed to fade away. I reckon he *died* _____ *a broken heart.*

c He finally *died* yesterday _____ *a long illness.*

d She went peacefully. She *died* _____ *her sleep.*

e He *died* _____ *the injuries* he received in the crash.

f There's no real reason. He just *died* _____ *old age.*

g I've always wanted to *die* _____ *my bed.*

h She *died* _____ *cancer.*

WORD FORMATION

Part A   Unit 7

11 Complete the chart.

Verb	Noun	Adjective	Past Participle
die			
live			
		xxxx	born

12 Fill the blanks with the right part of speech.

a He didn't have a horrible _____: it was quick, and seconds before he _____ he was laughing and joking.

b Here, he told me to give you his watch. It was his _____ wish.

c When anybody dies it is sad, but the _____ of children is the worst.

d I'll remember this moment to my _____ day.

e The _____ man lay undiscovered for some three weeks.

f The car engine spluttered and _____. We were stranded in a deserted country lane.

g _____ doesn't frighten me but making speeches does!

Which of the sentences have fixed phrases, and which use the word die, etc. metaphorically?

13 Which of these adjective are most likely to go with the following expressions? Sometimes more than one is possible.

> *deadly   fatal   lethal*

a She is suffering from a _____ illness.

b Who fired the _____ shot that killed the President?

c That's a _____ weapon!

d She took a _____ dose of poison and died.

e AIDS is a _____ virus.

f She took the _____ step which led to her death.

MEANING

Part A   Unit 1

📖 **14** Describe each of the incidents using one of the words or phrases in the box.

> to choke   to drown
> to have a heart attack
> to be run over
> to have a stroke
> to suffocate

"Divers today recovered the body of an old man from the river."

"Something she ate got stuck in her throat. There was absolutely nothing we could do."

"After the first one she was paralyzed all down one side. The second one killed her."

"He suddenly stood up and groaned. His face went all red and then he collapsed at our feet."

"That's the problem in most fires. People aren't burnt to death, they're overcome by the fumes."

"We think the accident took place sometime in the morning. We found the pedestrian lying in the road early this morning."

15 What other common forms of death can you think of apart from *to be murdered, to commit suicide,* and the words and expressions in exercises 10–12?

ACTIVATE

16 Deaths in fiction are many and varied. Here are some examples:

a Romeo and Juliet commit suicide.
b Dr Zhivago has a heart attack.
c Captain Ahab drowns.

What other fictional deaths can you think of?

METAPHOR & IDIOM

Part A   Unit 4

17 Read this passage from a story called "Maureen at the Factory Gates". Complete it with words from the box (you may have to change the form of the word).

> birth choke conceive
> death die drown
> heart attack pregnant

18 Can you think of the answers to these questions:

a What did the company make?
b What was Maureen's job?
c What was the chairwoman's idea which saved the company?

Does anyone have any ideas for saving this company? asked the chairwoman. There was a (1) _____ pause and then Valerie said what everyone had been thinking.

"We will have to shut down this company and start up somewhere else."

And so the plan was (2) _____.

"You don't have to come Madam Chairwoman," said Valerie two weeks later, at the end of what they thought would be their last meeting. But the chairwoman was adamant. "I helped to start this company," she said. " I was in at the (3) _____ and I might as well be in at the (4) _____.

So it was that on a windy day in March a sad group of workers gathered outside the main building to listen to Valerie say the words that would end the experiment they had begun. But even that was unsuccessful since most of her speech was (5) _____ out by the roadworks taking place outside the factory gates.

Of all the workers Maureen was the most upset and in her distress she started to cry. "I'm really (6) _____" she said. "I just don't know what to do."

But at that moment the noise of the drills on the road suddenly stopped and the sun came out. And the chairwoman stood up and made the suggestion that was to save them.

Many years later Maureen would describe her emotions on that day. "Well," she used to say, "I nearly had a (7) _____ when that woman told us what we were going to do. But it was worth it." And then she would turn to her husband and say "Have you got a fag? I'm (8) _____ for a smoke" and he would reply "You will if you have one." And they would both laugh.

19 Read this extract from an obituary.

Zamoro's work as a champion of the oppressed came to a sudden end when he had a stroke whilst on a visit to Rio de Janeiro. He died within a few hours. Doctors discovered that he had been suffering from a fatal illness and this probably provoked his death.

ACTIVATE

20 Write similar extracts about.

a a politician who was shot
b someone who died because they had an illness
c an old person who never woke up
d someone who died after a drug overdose
e someone who fell into a river
f someone whose heart stopped

21 Explain the newspaper headlines. Choose one and write the accompanying story.

Widow Sues Hotel Cook

MIRACLE OF FIRST BABY FOR PANDA HING-HING

Sextuplets Mum Ecstatic Says Proud Father

FATAL DISEASE THREATENS SEAL POPULATION

Distraught Romeo in Suicide Bid

FOCUS WORDS				
BIRTH AND DEATH	alive	dead = very	kill	quadruplets
	baby	deadly	labour	quintuplets
	bereaved	death	lethal	run over (v)
	birth	die	life	sextuplets
	caesarian	drown	live	suffocate (v)
	choke (v)	fatal	obituary	triplets
	conceive	funeral	pass away (v)	twins
	contractions	identical	pregnant	widow
	dead (adj)	(twins)		

FOCUS PHRASES

at peace
be born
become pregnant
be burnt to death
be expecting
be murdered
be overcome by fumes
commit suicide
the deceased

die of ⎡ natural causes
          ⎢ a broken heart
          ⎣ old age
die in your sleep
give birth to
give up the ghost
have a ⎡ heart attack
        ⎣ stroke
kick the bucket

8 *Waking and sleeping*

MEANING

1 In groups (and using dictionaries if necessary) check that you understand the meaning of all the words *in italics* in this questionnaire:

2 Complete the questionnaire in pairs.

3 Compare your results in groups.

SLEEP QUESTIONNAIRE

1 What is the first thing you do when you *wake up*?
_____

the last thing you do before you *go to sleep*?
_____

2 How many hour's sleep a night do you need?
_____

3 Do you sleep during the day (*naps, siestas, etc?*)

never	sometimes	often	always

4 Tick the correct box. Are you a *light sleeper?* ☐
heavy sleeper? ☐

5 Do you do any of the following?

	never	sometimes	often	always
snore				
sleepwalk				
talk in your sleep				
grind your teeth				

6 Which do you find the most irritating in other people?
_____

7 How often do you *dream?* *have nightmares?*

	never	sometimes	often	always

8 How did you sleep last night? Tick the appropriate boxes

I *fell into a deep sleep* immediately. ☐
was *tossing and turning* all night. ☐
slept like a log. ☐
couldn't *get to sleep.* ☐
kept *waking up.* ☐
woke up in the middle of the night
and couldn't *get back to sleep.* ☐
overslept. ☐

4 Read this extract from 'The Rider'. It is after lunch on a December afternoon.

5 Using the text and your imagination, describe the room. What type of people are these? What period is it? What is going to happen next?

Sarah was clearly *daydreaming* as she always did. Lloyd appeared to be *in a trance*, almost as if he was meditating. Old George had *dozed off* and even the duke was feeling *drowsy* as the remains of the winter sun warmed the room and the fire roared in the grate. Mrs Middle *yawned* loudly and then continued with her *forty winks*. Only Vivian was *alert*, sensing powerfully that something terrible was about to happen. Thus she was the first one to notice the black shape of the rider flash past the window.

MEANING IN CONTEXT

Part A Unit 1

6 Look at the phrases *in italics* in the text. Write the names of the characters in the chart. Use a dictionary to help you.

Awake	Asleep

7 Which characters could these words refer to?

conscious reverie catnap

WORD USE

COLLOCATIONS
Part A   Unit 5

📖**8** Which of these words go together? Tick the boxes.

	asleep	awake	alert	conscious
wide				
fast				
fully				
sound				
half				
semi-				

ACTIVATE

9 Use as much language as possible from the unit to describe the people in the pictures.

10 Use words from the unit to describe one of the following:

a a night you didn't get much sleep

b a time you had to use a lack of sleep as an excuse

c a time you did well despite a lack of sleep

d a time you overslept

e a time you fell asleep in strange surroundings

WORD FORMATION

PARTS OF SPEECH
Part A Unit 7

11 Make the following into adjectives that can come before a noun. You may have to add a word to some of them.

> sleep wake dream nightmare doze trance

12 Put the correct form of the word in the blanks.

a He looked at the _____ (*sleep*) child and felt reassured.

b The last three weeks had been a _____ (*wake*) nightmare as the little girl struggled to survive.

c He had been plagued with _____ (*nightmare*) thoughts about how he would explain it all to her.

d When he sat down to watch TV he fell into a _____ (*dream*) state where he was neither asleep nor awake.

e He was roused out of this _____ (*trance*) existence by the voice of his daughter. 'Don't worry, Daddy,' she said, 'it wasn't your fault.'

f That night he had no nightmares or visions. He fell into a _____ (*dream*) sleep the moment he hit the pillow and somehow everything was soon all right.

WORD USE

METAPHOR
Part A Unit 4

13 Put one of the following words in the blanks. You may have to change the form of the word.

> sleep wake up
> dream nightmare

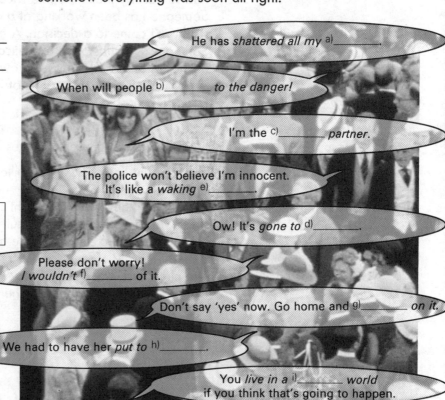

He has *shattered all my* a)_____ .

When will people b)_____ *to the danger!*

I'm the c)_____ *partner.*

The police won't believe I'm innocent. It's like a *waking* e)_____ .

Ow! It's *gone to* d)_____ .

Please don't worry! *I wouldn't* f)_____ of it.

Don't say 'yes' now. Go home and g)_____ *on it.*

We had to have her *put to* h)_____ .

You *live in a* i)_____ *world* if you think that's going to happen.

Why don't you go home and j)_____ *it off!*

14 Match the sentences from exercise 13 with the following ones:

a The vet destroyed our dog.
b The situation is unbearable.
c Don't make a decision now. Have a think about it.
d Part of my body has gone numb.
e I put my money in the company but I don't do anything else for it.
f Someone has completely disillusioned me.
g Go away – you're drunk!
h You don't have a good grasp of reality.
i People don't realise the seriousness of the situation.
j I promise I won't do it.

ACTIVATE

15 Write a dialogue about one of the following situations. Use as many of the expressions from exercise 13 as possible.

a At a party someone is drinking too much because they have had to destroy their valuable racehorse.
b Someone has been working at a computer screen all day and still hasn't come to a decision. A friend advises them.
c Someone who has been a political prisoner is celebrating his/her release and the overthrow of a dictator.
d A politician is denying reports of involvement in a company fraud to a probing journalist.

16 Use any two of these sentences in a story.

a The moment her head hit the pillow she fell into a deep and dreamless sleep.
b It was lucky they were such light sleepers.
c Sleepwalking obviously didn't suit him.
d Having her put to sleep was the hardest thing he had ever done.
e The nightmare was finally over.
f Daydreaming was something she would have to get used to!

FOCUS WORDS
WAKING AND SLEEPING

alert
asleep (fast asleep/
  half asleep/sound
  asleep)
awake (wide awake/
  half awake/fully
  awake)
catnap
consciousness (fully
  conscious/semi-
  conscious)
daydream

doze (off) (*v*)
dozy
drowsy
dream
dreamless
dream-like
dreamworld
forty winks
grind (your teeth)
nap
nightmare
oversleep

siesta
sleep (*v*)
sleeper (heavy/light
  sleeper)
sleeping (*adj*)
sleepwalk (*v*)
snore (*v*)
trance
trance-like
waking
wake up
yawn

FOCUS PHRASES

I wouldn't dream of it
fall into a deep sleep
go to sleep
put (an animal) to sleep
shatter all (my) dreams
sleep on it

sleep it off
sleeping partner
talk in your sleep
toss and turn
sleep like a log
waking nightmare

📖1 Using a dictionary or any other source, find out the meaning of these words.

> hangover   jogger   sidewalk   tailcoat   Bourbon
> archery   target   fog   klaxon   limped   fell

2 Look at these book covers. Based on the words in exercise 1, which do you think is likely to be the correct one for *Archery Target*?

Archery Target

A manual for sports lovers

Archery Target (An Inspector Polatski mystery)

No one is safe on the mean streets of New York

ARCHERY TARGET

A tale of adventure in medieval England

Archery Target (A Castle Hill Romance)

Did she love him or was it only his boats and his planes?

3 Read the text. Did you choose the correct book cover?

Archery Target

When I opened my eyes that morning I knew I should have stayed asleep. My head felt terrible, and when I got up it felt worse.

I lit a cigarette and dragged the electric razor across my chin. The noise it made hit the hangover in my brain like the *Dies Irae* from Verdi's *Requiem* – that's the bit with the bass drum, the shrieking chorus, and the full orchestra for those of you who don't know your Verdi. I hadn't managed to sleep it off after all. It was going to be one hell of a day.

As I opened the door the sunlight blasted into my eyes like a searchlight. It hurt. So did the jogger who sprinted past me as I stumbled into the street. I should have realised then that something was wrong. We didn't get many joggers in our neighbourhood – certainly not ones with bright-green running suits.

I staggered down towards the coffee shop for my morning coffee. I was moving at a snail's pace, but even that was faster than Easy Eddie who I met shuffling along the sidewalk. He was always shuffling along the sidewalk and I had got used to him by now. He gave me a cheerful greeting. I muttered, 'Hi'.

Someone strode past me and hurried down the street. He wasn't wearing a running suit, he was wearing a morning suit – with a tail coat and a white bow tie. I reckoned I must be hallucinating. For the hundredth time I swore I'd never drink Bourbon again.

I turned into Mission Boulevard and there she was. She was sauntering along on the other side of the street, colored like an archery target, with head held high and that innocent look of hers. Then, from the corner of my eye, I saw the running suit again and suddenly the fog blew right out of my head. *I knew what was going to happen!* I dashed across the road, weaving in and out of the early taxis and the garbage trucks as they hit their klaxons and shouted curses at me. But I was too late. I just had time to see the jogger stop her and the man with the morning suit touch her back – almost gently – and then they were gone.

'Lauren, Lauren,' I called through dry lips. She seemed to hear. She turned her head in my direction and limped towards me and then she just kind of fell in a rustling heap right there on the sidewalk. By the time I reached her she was gone.

I pulled another cigarette from the crushed packet in my pocket. One day, I swore, I'd give them up, but not now. Especially not now.

4 What image of the narrator do you have from reading the text? What do you think he is wearing?

5 The police want to interview people about the fatal attack on the woman. They are talking to either:

a a witness
b the jogger
c the narrator

In pairs, conduct the interviews. You can add any details that you think fit into the story.

MEANING IN CONTEXT

📖**6** Put these words or phrases from the text in the correct columns.

| sprinted | staggered | stumbled | shuffling |
| strode | sauntering | dashed | limped |

	Walk	Run
slowly and with difficulty		
trying not to make a noise		
looking ridiculous and/ or clumsy		
in a showing-off kind of way		
showing anger or strong decision		
slowly and with pleasure		
as fast as possible		
at a reasonable speed for training		

📖**7** Using a dictionary if necessary, add these words to the chart.

| jog plod stroll wander strut swagger stomp pad tiptoe waddle lurch totter hobble creep sidle march pace |

ACTIVATE

8 Use some of the walking and running verbs in sentences describing the situations listed here.

a A man approaches a woman in an over-friendly way.

b A woman is late and is trying not to miss her train.

c A man has been hit by a bullet but is nevertheless trying to reach his house.

d A poet is walking through the countryside in a dream.

e A young woman is trying to leave the house without her parents hearing her.

f A man walks into his boss's office intending to have an argument with him.

g Two girls run out of school, anxious to be home in time to watch a soap opera on the TV.

h A man is in the corridor outside the room where his wife is giving birth.

i A woman has been drinking a lot when she hears a knock at the door.

WORD USE

COLLOCATION
Part A   Unit 5

9 Put the walking verbs from exercises 6 and 7 in the correct box in the diagram to show which adverb they collocate with. Where there is more than one possibility put the words in more than one box.

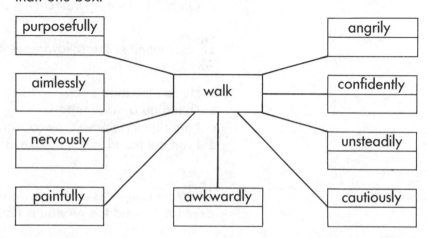

purposefully		angrily
aimlessly	**walk**	confidently
nervously		unsteadily
painfully	awkwardly	cautiously

ACTIVATE

10 Look at the photographs and complete the tasks.

a Give the people names.

b Give their ages and say what their occupations might be.

c Using adverbs as well as verbs, describe how the people usually walk.

WORD GRAMMAR

PHRASAL VERBS
Part A   Unit 11

11 Rewrite the following sentences using one of these phrasal verbs.

> run over   run into   run up   run out of
> run away from   run out

a I'm escaping from my parents.
b I met my cousin by accident in the High Street.
c Oh no, we haven't got any sugar left!
d They made the sheriff leave the town.
e I'll make you a skirt really quickly.
f Oh no! Did we hit that cat?

12 Say whether the following sentences are correct or not and why.

a He ran the man over.
b I'll run up a quick report.
c I am running my wife away from.
d I ran my friend into the other day.

ACTIVATE

13 Write sentences of your own using the phrasal verbs from exercise 11 and the pronouns *I* and *we*.

WORD USE

METAPHOR AND IDIOM
Part A   Unit 4

14 Identify the idiomatic expressions in the following sentences. Are they related to running or walking? What do you think each means?

a When I saw the look in his eyes it made my blood run cold. I knew that something terrible had happened.
b This play will run and run! People will be talking about it for years.
c Before you make a decision I think you should just run your eyes over this document.
d She's so much cleverer than her brother. She just runs rings round him.
e You shouldn't let her walk all over you like that. You should stand up for yourself a bit.
f If you don't supervise the children properly, Mr Chivers, they'll just run riot.
g He's such a fool. He should have known what was coming but he just walked right into it.

Check the meanings in your dictionary. Were you correct?

15 Write about one of the following topics using at least two expressions from exercise 14.

a A journalist has been made a fool of by a clever politician.
b A young man's girlfriend has been cheating on him and he is talking to his mother.
c A woman talks of the time she was nearly killed by a group of revolutionaries.

MEANING

Part A Unit 1

16 Match the animals with the sentences

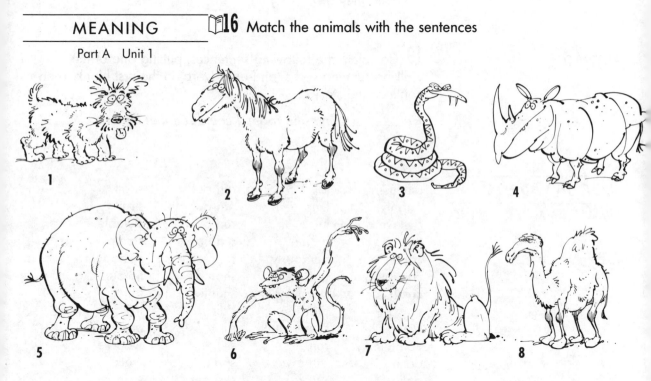

1
2
3
4
5
6
7
8

a It *cantered* up to the fence.
b It *trotted* along by its master's side.
c It *hopped* from the branch onto the roof of the car.
d It *crashed* through the undergrowth straight towards the photographer.
e Riderless, it *galloped* off into the sunset, past the pyramids, out into the desert.
f It *bounded* up to him, with eager anticipation.
g Suddenly I saw it, *slithering* through the leaves.
h It *padded* softly towards the unsuspecting antelope.

Can you describe the movement that the animal is making in each sentence?

ACTIVATE

17 Can you think of any people who might run or walk in the ways described in exercise 16? Write sentences about them.

GAME

18 One team thinks of a well-known person. The other team has to guess who it is by asking questions like the following.

a If this person was an animal what animal would they be?
b If this person was walking how would they walk?
c If this person was a form of transport what form of transport would they be?

ACTIVATE

19 Complete the following sentences, putting one of the walking/running verbs (and an adverb) in the first blank. Then continue the story.

He _____ into the room. I could see that he was _____ .

FOCUS WORDS

WALKING AND RUNNING

aimlessly	jog	run out	stroll
angrily	limp	run out of	strut
awkwardly	lurch	run over	stumble
bound	march	run up	stomp
canter	nervously	saunter	swagger
cautiously	pad	shamble	tiptoe
crash	painfully	shuffle	totter
crawl	plod	sidle	trot
creep	purposefully	slink	unsteadily
confidently	run	slither	waddle
dash	run away	sprint	walk
gallop	from	stagger	wander
hobble	run in	stride	weave
hop	run into		

FOCUS PHRASES

make (my) blood run cold
move at a snail's pace
run and run
run (your) eyes over this

run rings round
run riot
walk all over (you)
walk right into it

|10| *Body language and movement*

MEANING

Part A   Unit 1

1 Look at the pictures. Which people are *bowing, kneeling* or *curtsying*? Why are they doing it?

a
b
c
d
e
f

2 What would you be expected to do if you came face to face with one of the following people? What would you do?

a The Prime Minister of your country.
b The Queen of England.
c A religious leader.
d Your favourite film star.
e The national beauty queen.

3 Which of the following parts of the body can go with these verbs? One verb often goes with more than one part of the body and vice versa.

> head   fist   finger   hands   arm(s)   leg(s)   eyebrow(s)
> hand   shoulders   hips   teeth   ear(s)

a wave _____
b incline _____
c clench _____
d point _____
e wiggle _____
f wag _____
g fold _____
h hunch _____
i shrug _____
j nod _____
k raise _____
l cross _____
m shake _____

4 Use the verbs from exercise 3 in these sentences.

a 'Get out of here!' he said through _____ teeth.

b She _____ her fist at the departing policemen.

c She _____ her head vigorously but she was unable to say 'Yes' out loud.

d He _____ his shoulders: he didn't care anyway.

e The teacher ignored her even when she _____ her hand.

f He _____ his eyebrows at the unexpected news.

g He _____ his arms and prepared to endure another lecture.

5 Which of the expressions in exercise 3 denote the following? (People from different cultures may differ in their interpretations, of course.)

a expressing surprise
b expressing anger
c seeking attention
d expressing boredom
e agreeing
f being sexually provocative
g expressing indifference

ACTIVATE

6 Complete the questionnaire in pairs or groups.

What actions or gestures do you use to do the following?

INTERVIEWEE NUMBER	1	2	3	4
say hello				
say goodbye				
express anger				
express surprise				
express indifference				
express agreement				
express disagreement				

Do people from different cultures do any of these things differently?

7 In groups discuss what the people in the pictures are doing and what feelings they are trying to convey.

8 Are you left-handed or right-handed? Say which hand, arm, leg or thumb is used or is on top when you do the following.

INTERVIEWEE NUMBER	1	2	3	4	5
write					
clap					
cross your fingers					
fold your arms					
put your arms behind your back					
scratch your back					
cross your legs					

Do these actions the other way round: is it difficult?

MEANING IN CONTEXT

Part A   Unit 1

9 Look at the picture and read the text. Write the names of the characters in the story against the correct number.

1 _____
2 _____
3 _____
4 _____
5 _____
6 _____
7 _____
8 _____
9 _____

The first thing I noticed as I walked into the room was Jim *on his hands and knees* looking for something under the sofa. On it was Sara, *sitting stiffly* and looking into the middle distance. Peregrine was *lounging* against the book shelf, of course, and Pamela was *slouched* in the armchair. There was a strained silence in the room. Martin was *bending over* the little chest whilst Caroline was *flat on her back* under the table. The Colonel *stood erect* looking terribly serious.

From the bench by the window there came the sound of muffled sobbing. Jessica sat *with her head in her hands* and Mary sat unblinking, *hugging her knees*, humming softly to herself.

At that moment Caroline spoke.

'Isn't anyone else going to help? We'll never find it unless some of you join in.'

Then she saw me and went silent.

'In God's name,' I said, 'what's going on? What is it that you are looking for?'

Now answer the narrator's question!

ACTIVATE

10 Complete the questionnaire about yourself and about others.

> How do you sit or stand when you are doing the following?
>
> having breakfast _____
> at a friend's party _____
> watching television _____
> listening to music through headphones _____
> having tea/coffee with a distant relation _____
> puzzling over a problem when sitting down _____
> cleaning a stain from the carpet _____

MEANING

Part A Unit 1

11 Read this description and put the verbs in the correct blanks.

> *carry   push   pull   drag   stretch   reach*

John wanted to play with his train set, but it was in its case on a high shelf. He a)_____ the desk against the wall. Then he b)_____ a box over to the desk and put it on the top of it. He stood on the box and c)_____ up to the shelf. By d)_____ his fingers to their maximum extent he could just get hold of a handle of the case. He e)_____ it towards him. It came off the shelf suddenly and fell crashing to the floor. It was heavier than he had expected and he couldn't lift it. He f)_____ it towards the door.

ACTIVATE

12 Using the verbs from exercise 11 explain how you would do these actions.

a Get an impossibly heavy suitcase from your flat to the station.

b Change a bulb in a light which is hanging from a very high ceiling. You do not have a step ladder.

c Survive and get rescued after your plane has crashed into the jungle.

MEANING

METAPHOR AND IDIOM
Part A   Unit 4

13 Put the correct form of the following verbs in the blanks.

bow	bend	reach
pull	push	drag

I will not have you a)_____ her name through the mud. She's done nothing to deserve it.

I've b)_____ over backwards to help you.

Don't c)_____ for the stars too early in your career!

Don't d)_____ me too far or I might lose my temper!

He felt himself being e)_____ in two different directions.

I'm sure we could f)_____ an agreement on this.

I g)_____ to your judgement. I'll agree to the deal.

14 Match the phrases in exercise 13 with these explanations.

a I trust your superior sense.
b I've done everything I can – and more.
c We could agree in the end.
d I won't allow you to ruin her reputation.
e Don't provoke me.
f Don't be too ambitious.
g People with different opinions were trying to get his agreement.

ACTIVATE

15 Read the following resumé of a story.

Write the dialogue in the bar between Cartwright and Franklin. Use phrases from exercise 13.

Randy Cartwright is managing director of a company that makes aeroplane engines. Dan Franklin is his assistant. Franklin knows that Cartwright has been selling engine parts to terrorists (illegaly) and that company money has been used to fund the Moratovian Liberation Group (the MLG). Franklin has said that he will go to the newspapers with the story. Cartwright likes Franklin (he is married to Franklin's sister) and wants to head him off. They meet in an anonymous bar to discuss the situation.

FOCUS WORDS

USING DIFFERENT PARTS OF THE BODY/USING TOOLS

bend over
bow (v)
carry
carve
clench (your fist/teeth)
cross (your arms/legs)
curtsy
drag (v)
(stand) erect
fold (your arms)
hunch (your shoulders)
incline (your head)
kneel
lounge (v)
nod your head

point (a finger)
pull
push
raise (your hand/arm)
reach (v)
shake (your fist/head)
shrug (your shoulders)
slouch (v)
(sit) stiffly
stand
stretch (v)
wag (your finger)
wave (your arms/hand)
wiggle (your hips)

FOCUS PHRASES

be pulled in two/both directions
bow to (your) judgement
drag someone's name through the mud
be flat on (your) back
hug (your) knees

on (your) hands and knees
push someone too far
reach an agreement
reach for the stars/moon
with (your) head in (your) hands
bend over backwards

The mind and thinking

1 Think about these questions and try to answer them:

a Where is your brain, and where is your mind?
b Do you think with your mind or your brain?
c Do you feel emotions with your brain or your mind?
d Which works harder for you, your mind or your brain? Why?

Compare your answers with a partner's.

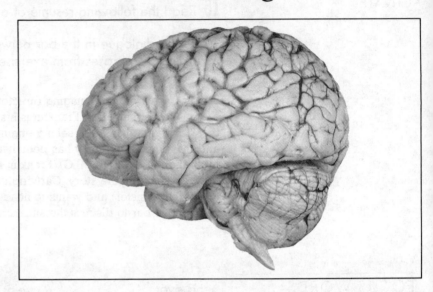

MEANING

SENSE RELATIONS
Part A Unit 3

2 Put each verb from the following sentences in the correct box on page 119. Then discuss your answers with a partner.

a The children were trying to *guess* my age.
b It's reasonable to *suppose* that they've hidden the money somewhere.
c They *assessed* the results of the experiment carefully.
d George *pondered* his future with a heavy heart.
e I think we can safely *assume* that they will agree to our terms.
f It's time to *analyse* these statistics to see what they mean.
g What did you *conclude* from her speech?
h There were three dignitaries to *judge* the contestants' work.
i The prisoners were left to *reflect* on their crimes.
j I *infer* from Ms Jones's remarks that she is against the plan.
k Jane's been *considering* the options open to her for some time.
l They *weighed up* the consequences of taking out another loan.
m We've been *deliberating* for days; we'll have to make a decision soon.
n I *reckon* it's going to rain pretty soon.
o The accountant is trying to *work out* how much tax Liz owes.
p The guru spends much of the day *meditating*.

Think about something carefully and for a long time, without necessarily coming to a conclusion.
Come to a tentative conclusion about something, based on limited evidence and maybe personal opinion.
Come to a conclusion about something after examining all the evidence and facts.
Find out by scientific examination or calculation.

WORD GRAMMAR

VERB COMPLEMENTATION
Part A   Unit 12

Put *T* beside any of the verbs from exercise 2 that can be immediately followed by an object (i.e. any that are transitive). Put the most useful *preposition* beside the others.

WORD USE

STYLE
Part A   Unit 6

3 Which of the verbs are *formal*, which *informal*, and which *neutral* in style? Mark them *F, I* and *N*.

WORD FORMATION 📖 4

VERBS, NOUNS AND ADJECTIVES
Part A   Unit 7

a Which of the verbs in exercise 2 can be turned into nouns using the following endings? Write the nouns down and try to compose suitable examples for each.

-tion/-sion	-ence	-ing	-ment

b Which can be turned into adjectives using the ending *-ive*? What does each *-ive* adjective mean?

ACTIVATE

📖**5** Read the following sentences. Then for each construct a new sentence with the same meaning using the words indicated.

Example Is it a safe assumption that the train will be on time? *assume*
→ Can we safely assume that the train will be on time?

a Was it your impression that the experiment had failed? *conclude*

b Who carried out the analysis of the results? *analyse*

c Jane thought deeply about the implications of the changes. *ponder*

d We gave the matter a lot of thought. *consider*

e The calculation took him a long time. *work (it) out*

f He seemed to be deep in thought. *meditate*

g What inference can we draw from this discussion? *infer*

h Diana has probably gone to see Andy. *suppose*

i After thinking it over for a few days, Sally accepted the job. *reflection*

6 Read these quotations. Which do you like best, and why? Which don't you agree with? Discuss your answers with a partner.

> *What we call a mind is nothing but a heap or collection of different perceptions, united together by certain relations and supposed, though falsely, to be endowed with a perfect simplicity and identity.*   (David Hume)

> **You cannot think about thinking, without thinking about thinking about something.**   (Seymour Papert)

> *Mind — a mysterious form of matter secreted by the brain. Its chief activity consists in the endeavour to ascertain its own nature, the futility of the attempt being due to the fact that it has nothing but itself to know itself with.*   (Ambrose Biercel)
>
> *The hardest thing to understand is why we can understand anything at all.*   (Albert Einstein)

What is your definition of 'mind'? Can you and your partner make up another 'quotation' about the workings of the mind?

MEANING

RELATED MEANINGS
Part A Unit 2

📖**7** Complete the following using an appropriate word from the box in each case.

> *mind   intelligence   mentality   brain   idea*
> *impression   thought   logic   notion   memory*

a A: Is that puzzle difficult?
  B: It is for me. My _____ is not used to working out problems of _____ any more.
  A: Well, it does say 'Puzzles for people of above average _____'!

b C: Mum, what's the difference between philosophy and psychology?
  D: Well, philosophy is the study of the history and present state of human _____, and psychology is the study of how the human _____ works. Why?
  C: I can't spell either of them.

c E: George has some rather strange _____.
  F: Why do you say that? I've only met him twice, but he made rather a good _____ on me.
  E: Well, he firmly believes that the earth is flat, and refuses to accept the _____ that it is round. And he's not joking.
  F: Some people have a peculiar _____, don't they.

d G: Did you post the letters?
  H: Oh, no, I forgot. My _____ is getting terrible.

MEANING IN
CONTEXT

MEANING
Part A   Unit 1

8 Try to find an equivalent for each of the expressions *in italics*:

a A: Let's go out tonight.
   B: What *did you have in mind*?

b C: I can't *make up my mind* what to do.
   D: Why don't you get some advice from a lawyer?

c E: What are we going to do about these noisy neighbours?
   F: It's after midnight now. *I've got a good mind* to call the police.

d G: You look pensive.
   H: Mmm. *I've got something on my mind.*
   G: Do you want to talk about it?

e J: We've run out of bread. *Would you mind* going to get some?
   K: All right — if you give me the money.

f L: Look, there's a parking space on the other side of the road.
   M: *Mind out*, there's a car coming.

g N: I think I'm going to fail the maths exam tomorrow.
   O: I'm sure you can pass if you *put your mind to it*.

ACTIVATE

9 With a partner make up a brief dialogue using any three of the expressions in exercise 7.

10 What do you think these three sayings mean? Are they true, in your experience?

"Out of sight, out of mind."

"Mind over matter."

"Great minds think alike."

📖**11** In the table below, indicate whether a word can be used to describe a person or an idea by putting a tick (√) in the appropriate columns.

	Person	Idea
logical		
pensive		
thoughtful		
thoughtless		
aware		
reasonable		
unreasonable		
mental		
psychological		
brainy		
brainless		
conceptual		
conscious		
unconscious		
intelligent		
intellectual		
considerate		
clever		

List three words from the table which can be used to describe the way a person treats other people, and two words which have a similar meaning to *intelligent*.

12 Which of the adjectives in the box in exercise 11 can be used in which of the following sentence frames? More than one word can be used in many of the sentences, and the same word can sometimes be used in different sentences.

a You look _____. What are you thinking about?
b It was very _____ of you to warm the room for me. Thank you.
c The patients here are all suffering from _____ illness of one kind or another.
d As she woke up, Rebecca was _____ of a presence near the bed.
e Those twins are very _____. They've already passed the advanced exams in maths.
f That was a(n) _____ thing to say. Now she's upset.
g The Greens paid a(n) _____ price for the house.
h After the fight, he fell _____ to the floor.
i I couldn't understand their arguments: they were(not) _____.

WORD USE

IDIOM
Part A   Unit 4

13 The two dialogues below have got mixed up after the first line. Put them in the correct order.

a

1. I have *lovely memories* of our college days.

☐ What do you mean: it's possible that I'm right? Here's a photo of you at the bottom of the stairs as a *permanent reminder*.

☐ Don't *you remember*? She had dark hair and brown eyes. A real beauty *if my memory serves me well*.

☐ *I'll never forget* the day you got drunk and fell down the stairs, for example.

☐ I need something to *jog my memory*. What was Angela like?

☐ Really? Down the stairs? I *have no recollection* of the incident.

☐ *My mind's a blank*, but it's possible that you're right.

☐ Yes, me too. Whenever we meet it all *comes back to me*.

☐ You were in love with someone called Angela, *as I recall*. That's what caused it.

b

1. Hallo. Didn't you say you would meet us at 6.30? Or *is my memory playing tricks*?

☐ By the way, I was *racking my brains* trying to think of Joe's surname. What is it?

☐ And where's Joe? I hope he hasn't forgotten all about the meeting. He's so *absent-minded* these days.

☐ It looks as if no one has remembered to bring it. What a *memorable* meeting we're having.

☐ Perhaps we'd better phone to *remind* him. Who can remember his phone number?

☐ Erm . . . it's *on the tip of my tongue*: Donaldson or Davison I think.

☐ It's getting really late now. Where can he be? He's so *forgetful*.

☐ Did I? I've got *a mind like a sieve*, I'm afraid. I thought I said 7 o'clock.

List words and expressions from the two dialogues in the correct boxes.

Remembers/remembered	Doesn't/didn't remember

14 Do you have a good memory or a bad memory? Use some of the words and expressions from exercise 13 to tell a partner about two of the most memorable experiences in your life, good or bad!

FOCUS WORDS
THE MIND AND THINKING

absent-minded
analyse/analysis
assess/assessment
assume/assumption
aware/awareness
brain/brainy/brainless
clever/cleverness
concept/conceptual
conclude/conclusion
conscious/unconscious/
    consciousness
consider/considerate/
    consideration
deliberate/deliberation
forget/forgetful
guess
idea/idealistic
impression/impressive
infer/inference
intellect/intellectual
intelligent/intelligence

judge/judgement
logic/logical
meditate/meditation
memory/memorable
mental/mentality
mind
notion/notional
pensive
ponder
psychology/psychological
reason/reasonable/
    unreasonable
recall
reckon/reckoning
reflect/reflection
remind/reminder
suppose/supposition
thought/thoughtful/
    thoughtless
weigh up
work out

FOCUS PHRASES

as I recall
great minds think alike
have a mind like a sieve
have no recollection
if my memory serves me well
it all comes back (to me)
jog someone's memory
mind over matter

(my) memory is playing tricks
(my) mind is a blank
on the tip of (my) tongue
out of sight out of mind
permanent reminder
rack (your) brains
remember as if it was
    yesterday

1 Look at this diagram. What can you see?
How many triangles are there in the diagram?
How many circles or discs are there?
Where are the circles in relation to the triangles?

Compare your answers with a partner's.

The Kanizsa Triangle

2 Read the text. Find out what 'Gestalt' means.

Can you think of other images which have a similar effect? Do you agree with this theory of perception? If not, why not?

'Why do things look as they do?' This, suggested the psychologist Koffka, is the basic question for any theory of perception. And, moreover, the answer must be sought by finding out how things do look. To me the diagram above looks like an erect white triangle superimposed upon, and somewhat in front of, an inverted triangle outlined in black, with a black disc beneath each corner of the white triangle.

By simple elegant demonstrations of this kind, the Gestalt psychologists showed that things do not look as they do because they are what they are. There are no triangles in the figure, and certainly not a white one standing in front of the page. Nor for that matter are there any circles. So what is the basis for our perceptual experiences? Since there are no triangles or circles in the figure there is the problem of explaining how the sensory input from it could ever become associated with images of triangles and circles. To the Gestalt psychologists the solution was that the processes in the brain, present at birth, must be responsible for the way we see the world.

(adapted from Open University D303 Unit 6 p.16)

WORD FORMATION

NOUNS, ADJECTIVES AND
VERBS
Part A   Unit 7

3 Complete this table of words from the text. Circle the new words if they have a very different meaning.

Nouns	Adjectives	Verbs
psychologist theory perception		xxxxx
	outlined	
demonstration experience		
	sensory	
image process		

MEANING

Part A   Unit 2

4 Which of the words in the completed table in exercise 3 means:

a to show that something is true
b a system or method of doing something
c relating to ideas which might explain observed facts
d to see, hear, smell, taste or touch something
e a picture or design of any kind

WORD USE

COLLOCATION
Part A   Unit 5

5 Select the appropriate verb for each of the following examples and say why it is appropriate.

a We were walking home one night and suddenly we (saw/looked at) a shooting star.

b A: What are you (seeing/looking at)?
B: I'm just (seeing/watching) those birds building a nest.

c I don't (see/watch) television much these days.

d C: (See/Look at) those men. They're climbing through your window.
D: Where? I can't (see/watch) them.

e E: Ssh. Did you (hear/listen to) that noise upstairs?
F: Yes. (Hear/Listen): there it is again. Let's go and (see/look at) what's happening.

f By coincidence I (saw/looked at) my ex-husband in the street yesterday. He (saw/looked at) me as if I was a ghost!

Which of these verbs normally imply conscious attention?

MEANING

SENSE RELATIONS
Part A   Unit 3

📖 **6** In each of these examples, there is a different verb of *looking* or *seeing*. Using a dictionary if necessary, find a suitable ending for each of the incomplete sentences.

a	She stared	1	the red Mercedes as it flashed by.
b	She glanced	2	at the building through the fog.
c	She gazed	3	a small crack she hadn't seen before.
d	She observed	4	at him in absolute horror.
e	She noticed	5	through a crack in the door to see inside.
f	She spotted	6	at him quickly to see if he had heard.
g	She scanned	7	a face she recognised in the crowd.
h	She peered	8	at him in deep admiration.
i	She peeped	9	the people on the beach below carefully.
j	She glimpsed/ caught a glimpse of/ caught sight of	10	the pages of the newspaper in case there was a report on the meeting.

Mark the sentences L (= long duration), S (= short duration) or N (= neutral duration).

ACTIVATE

7 Use words from exercise 6 to tell the story outlined in these notes. Do **not** use *see* or *look*.

Mark needed to find a new flat / pages of the newspaper (for advertisements) / appointment to visit a flat / arrived at the building / up the stairs / young woman rushed past him / looked at him in shock / Mark just had time to see blood on her hand / ran up to the flat, knocked on door / no answer / looked through the keyhole / nothing unusual / but smelled smoke / broke down the door / tried to see across the room / (tears caused by smoke) / put out the fire in the kitchen / looked round the room in astonishment: chaos / went into the bedroom / looked with horror at the body on the floor: a man with a kitchen knife in his back in a pool of blood / saw by chance the phone under the bed / called the police / closed the eyes of the victim which looked penetratingly at him / Mark decided not to take this flat.

8 List some things which:

Taste	Feel	Smell	Look
sweet	soft	rotten	dangerous
sour	rough	sweet	ugly
salty	smooth	sweaty	frightening
hot (like chilli)	sticky	acrid	exciting
like vinegar	cold	like flowers	relaxing
	like silk		like cheese

9 Look at these five words describing different types of smell.

> *fragrance   stink   aroma   stench   perfume*

Put them in order from 1 (= most unpleasant) to 5 (= most pleasant). Use a dictionary to help you.

ACTIVATE

10 Complete the questionnaire in pairs, taking it in turns to ask and answer the questions. Use expressions like these.

> *the fragrance/aroma/stink/stench/smell of...*
> *the taste of...   the flavour of...   the way (something) tastes...*
> *the way (someone/something) looks...*
> *the sight of...   the view from...   the sound of...*
> *the noise (something) makes when...*

WHAT IS/ARE ...

the nicest sound you've ever heard (not including music)? _____

the most unbearable sound you've ever heard? _____

the most beautiful sight or view you've ever seen? _____

the most horrible sight you've ever seen? _____

the most delicious thing you've ever tasted? _____

the most revolting thing you've ever tasted? _____

the most wonderful aroma you've ever smelled? _____

the smell you've found it hardest to bear? _____

three things you really like the feel of? _____

MEANING

11 Put the boxed words (which have the same form for both noun and verb) into the appropriate column in the table. Indicate the degree of intensity of each word by putting 1 (not intense), 2 or 3 (very intense) beside it.

| shine bang glow flash roar knock pop dazzle |
| crash glint glimmer glitter bump rustle rumble |

You see them	You hear them

For each word, find an example of something that could make the noise or have the visual effect.

ACTIVATE

12 Which of the words in exercise 11 would you use with each of these subjects?

a thunder during a storm
b a cork coming out of a bottle
c fireworks at a festival
d silver fish in the sun
e a mouse among some papers
f lightning in the evening sky
g the headlights of a car
h somebody dropping a suitcase on a wooden floor
i an angry lion
j a stone smashing a window
k a small fire 100 metres away

WORD USE

METAPHOR AND IDIOM
Part A   Unit 4

13 Complete the following dialogue with phrases from the boxes.

keep an eye on
sight for sore eyes
you seem
it seems to me to/that
from my point of view
in my view
take a long-term view
the way I look at it

look(s) as if/as though
sound(s) as if/as though
have a nice/nasty feel to it
leave a nasty/sour taste
in your mouth
in bad/good/the best taste
smell a rat

A: What do you think of my new car then?

B: I must say, it's absolutely beautiful, _____.
It's a 1956 Jaguar, isn't it?

A: Yes. I _____ advertisements in the papers, just in case there's a car I really want. And this one suddenly popped up. It was a bargain.

B: It certainly _____ you've found what you were looking for. How much was it, if you don't mind my asking?

A: Only £8,000. _____, that was a reasonable price to pay.

B: £8,000 for an old car! You must have money to burn!

A: Well, you've got to _____: you've got to think of the future. It's better to buy a car which is going to increase in value than one which is going to lose value, in _____.

B: Is it really worth that much?

A: Yes. In fact, the owner wanted £9,000 for it to start with, because he said it had only done 60,000 miles. But I _____, and in the end he admitted that 160,000 was nearer the truth. So he dropped the price.

B: And what's it like to drive?

A: Lovely. It's got a nice solid _____.

B: I must say, I envy you. But spending that amount of money would certainly _____ in my mouth!

ACTIVATE

14 Imagine that, having lost your sight or your hearing as a child of five, you have just had an operation that has more or less restored your sight/hearing. Write an entry for your diary or a short article for a magazine. Use vocabulary from this unit.

FOCUS WORDS

aroma	image/ imagine	rumble
bang	knock	rustle
bump	listen	scan
crash	look	see
dazzle	look at	seem
demonstrate/	noise	sense/ sensory
demonstration/	notice	shine
demonstrative	observe	sight
experience	outline	smell
feel	peep	sound
flash	peer	spot
flavour	perceive/ perception/	stare
fragrance	perceptive	stench
gaze	perfume	stink
glance	pop	taste
gleam	process	theory/ theorize/
glimmer	psychology/	theoretical
glimpse	psychologist	thud
glint	recognize	view
glitter	roar	watch
glow		
hear		

FOCUS PHRASES

catch a glimpse of	leave a nice/nasty taste in
catch sight of	your mouth
from my point of view	look as if/as though
have a nice/nasty feel to it	sight for sore eyes
in bad/good/the best taste	smell a rat
in my view	sound as if/though
it seems to me that	take a long-term view
keep an eye on	the way I look at it

|13| *Feelings and moods*

1 Choose one of the words below as the title for this poem, and use the same word to fill the blanks.

> hope worry irritation
> happiness ecstasy

Do you like this poem? Why/why not?

Where would we be with without _____?
It helps keep the brain occupied.
Doing doesn't take your mind off things,
I've tried.

_____ is God's gift to the nervous.
Best if kept bottled up inside.
I once knew a man who couldn't care less.
He died.

Roger McGough

MEANING

Part A Unit 1

2 Put the listed words in the column which you think is most appropriate.

anguished	bored	ecstatic	scared
astounded	dismayed	horrified	astonished
depressed	heartbroken	pleased	delighted
glad	nervous	apprehensive	furious
miserable	upset	cross	livid
thrilled	appalled	frightened	terrified
anxious	concerned	irritated	

Happy	Unhappy	Worried	Angry	Afraid	Shocked

WORD FORMATION 📖3

PARTS OF SPEECH
Part A   Unit 7

Look at the words in exercise 2 again. Use a dictionary to find out whether they have an equivalent verb, and write *V* beside them if they do.

WORD FORMATION

SUFFIXES AND PREFIXES
Part A   Unit 8

4 Explain this cartoon. What is the first speaker's mistake?

This play is terrible. I am very boring.

Yes it is, and you are certainly boring, but not all the time.

Put the correct form of the adjective in these sentences.

a The paintings were very gruesome. I was (appall) _____.

b This play is extremely (upset) _____. I don't want to go on watching it.

c He makes me feel very (inhibit) _____. I don't feel able to express my feelings when he's around.

d The sight of an audience of 2,000 people as you get up to speak is very (intimidate) _____.

5 Re-write these sentences using *exactly* the word given.

a I cannot believe the news you have just given me. *astonishing*

b She felt her anger increasing with every word he uttered. *irritated*

c When I burst the balloon the poor child leapt nearly three feet into the air. *frightening*

d I can't help being very worried about the future. *anxiety*

e The puppet show made the children very happy. *delighted*

f I think about you all the time and then I feel unhappy. *worry*

g I am utterly shocked by his rude behaviour. *appalls*

h My heart is full of joy at your arrival. *gladdens*

ACTIVATE

6 Look at these people.

Say how you think they felt when they:

a got their exam results

b heard the news of an earthquake

c found out that they were going to be an aunt or uncle

d heard terrible laughter coming from the loft of their house in the middle of the night

e discovered that their friend had taken their car without asking and crashed it into a lorry

f found a note saying that their partner had gone off with another man/woman

g answered the door to find a man telling them that they had won a lottery

Choose one of the situations and make a conversation in which the person rings up their best friend to tell them about it.

7 Make a list of the kind of topics you would expect to find in a horoscope. What kind of predictions are usually given about those topics?

Topics	Predictions

8 Read this horoscope from a woman's magazine and answer these questions:

a Which of the topics you selected in exercise 7 are not mentioned here?

b Which topics mentioned here are not in your original list?

c Which of the predictions you suggested in exercise 7 are not given here?

d Which predictions in this horoscope are not in your original list?

e Which star sign is missing?

Your Horoscope

Lucille Burton

ARIES   *March 21 – April 19*
Your patience could be sorely tested – keep your temper under control. Money matters need to be thought through as precipitous action might cause anxiety. A child's input is surprisingly wise.

TAURUS   *April 20 – May 20*
Neighbours could provide a social life for you if you were not too unfriendly. Someone who's been critical of you is feeling inadequate herself. If you become defensive, you'll both feel guilty.

GEMINI   *May 21 – June 21*
A visit from an out-of-town relative needn't be a burden. Modify your attitudes. Don't procrastinate with a minor medical problem. A doctor's visit would relieve your mind.

CANCER   *June 22 – July 22*
Don't be stubborn; you must listen to a family member's point of view. A party or social situation will be a good place for making contacts. A financial adviser could mislead you, so get a second opinion before putting money on the line.

LEO   *July 23 – August 22*
Enjoy an expensive purchase. A sermon or conversation may inspire you to deep feelings of serenity. A loved one's well-meaning advice may be too fear-based, so trust your own instincts.

LIBRA   *September 23 – October 22*
You may be feeling impatient; guard temper and sensitivity. Money matters could be a mixed bag; some balance is coming. You'll need to be realistic about a friendship that has seen better days.

SCORPIO *October 23 – November 21*
You could be helpful to a neighbour without much effort. Keep better informed about current events if you want to socialise with interesting people. You may meet an old flame by accident. Don't be surprised if there's a touch of spark left.

SAGITTARIUS *November 22 – December 21*
You could be feeling nervous and shattered but this won't last. Make time for a physical sport you really enjoy. A young person's open-mindedness is to be commended. Don't let your fears inhibit you from doing what's right.

CAPRICORN *December 22 – January 19*
A change of scene would spark your enthusiasm; get away even for a day's outing. If friendship proves disappointing, focus on other things. Brooding won't help. Pay bills promptly.

AQUARIUS *January 20 – February 18*
You'll be in the limelight and enjoying favourable publicity. You could have trouble with an electrical gadget and would be wise to pay for professional repairs. Don't be intimidated by a smug female.

PISCES *February 19 – March 20*
Deep emotion could sweep over you for no apparent reason. It'll pass and you'll feel stronger. A pet should be taken to the vet if it becomes lethargic. Wise investment could now pay dividends.

9 Discuss the following:

a What is your star sign? Do any of Lucille Burton's predictions sound right for you?

b Do you normally read your horoscope? How much do you believe in it?

c What other ways of telling the future are there? Which do you have the most confidence in?

USING DICTIONARIES

DEFINITIONS
Book 2   Part A   Unit 1

10 Say when you might feel one of the emotions below. (They are all in the horoscope.) Use a dictionary to help you.

a unfriendly	**e** serene	**i** disappointed
b inadequate	**f** impatient	**j** intimidated
c guilty	**g** sensitive	**k** strong
d stubborn	**h** nervous	

11 What are the nouns which correspond to the adjectives in exercise 10?

12 Put an appropriate word or form of a word from exercise 10 in the blanks.

a When I arrived at the house he didn't even say hello to me. I thought he was very _____.
b You have to be very careful with her. If she's feeling _____ the slightest thing will make her cry.
c As she approached her death she gradually became more peaceful. Everyone remarked on her _____.
d When he asked for help again there was still nothing I could do and my feelings of _____ grew by the minute.
e You mustn't feel _____ just because he's your boss.
f Some men only buy their wives flowers when they are feeling _____ about something.
g Once she's made up her mind she won't budge. She's as _____ as a mule.
h Of course he felt _____ when he failed to get a place at the language school.

ACTIVATE

13 Write the entry for Virgo in the same style as Lucille Burton (Virgos are supposed to be perfectionists who want everything to be exactly right.)

14 In the horoscope for Aries it says 'keep your temper under control'.

Which of the following phrases go with *mood*, which phrases go with *temper*, and which phrases go with both? Tick the boxes.

		Mood	Temper
to be in a	good / bad / excellent / foul		
to	keep / lose your		

ACTIVATE

15 Describe someone you met recently who was in a particular mood and then nearly or completely lost their temper. What signs did they give of their mood or temper?

📖**16** Read these sentences.

WORD USE

METAPHOR AND IDIOM
Part A   Unit 4

Marina: It *made me really mad.*

Roger: It *got me down.*

Shiona: It really *gives me a buzz.*

Tom: It *took me completely by surprise.*

Will: I was *bowled over.*

Sarah: I was *caught off balance.*

Chris: I'm really *over the moon* about this.

Write the names of the speakers in the correct columns.

Happy	Surprised	Not happy

ACTIVATE

17 Look at the situations in exercise 6. Which of the expressions from exercise 16 could be used for those situations?

ACTIVATE

18 Interview your partner. Find out what they would most/least like to find in a horoscope.

Write their horoscope making predictions about the things they mentioned. Be sure to include love and money, and use as many words from this unit as possible.

FOCUS WORDS
MOODS AND FEELINGS

afraid	depressed	inadequate	scared
angry	disappointed	inhibit	sensitive
anguished	disappointing	inhibited	serene
anxiety	dismayed	inhibiting	serenity
anxious	ecstatic	interesting	shocked
appalled	ecstasy	intimidated	smug
appalling	frighten	irritated	strong
apprehensive	frightened	irritation	stubborn
astonished	furious	lethargic	surprise
astonishing	glad	livid	surprised
astounded	gladden	miserable	temper
attitude	guilty	mood	terrified
bored	happiness	nervous	thrilled
brooding	happy	opinion	unfriendly
cheer up	heartbroken	patience	unhappy
concerned	helpful	patient	upset
critical	hope	pleased	upsetting
cross	horrified	procrastinate	worried
defensive	impatient	relieved	worry
delighted			

FOCUS PHRASES

be in a good/bad mood
be interested in
be over the moon about
   something
bowl somebody over
catch somebody off balance

get somebody down
give somebody a buzz
keep/lose your temper
make somebody mad
take somebody by surprise

Likes and dislikes

1 Read this poem. Which of the following is it about?

a giving up smoking
b being in love
c liking music
d liking literature

NO SMOKING

Giving Up Smoking

There's not a Shakespeare sonnet
Or a Beethoven quartet
That's easier to like than you
Or harder to forget.

You think that sounds extravagant?
I haven't finished yet –
I like you more than I would like
to have a cigarette.

Wendy Cope

2 Which of the following things would you find most difficult to give up if you were asked to do so?

alcohol   smoking   meat   chocolate   something else

3 Read these comments and say which you sympathize with and why.

a I really *dislike* the habit.
b I would *hate* to think that a child of mine would start smoking.
c People seem to *detest* me just because I smoke. Well why not? I *like* smoking.
d I *don't care for* cigarettes. They are extremely unpleasant.
e I *get a kick out of* smoking. I'd just like to see someone try to stop me!
f I used to be a smoker, but now I've taken an intense *dislike* to the habit – it's distasteful and harmful.
g There's nothing I *loathe* more than people who've given up smoking. They're so self-righteous. I'm *not that keen on* it, but yes, I *enjoy* the occasional cigarette.
h I have a love-hate relationship with cigarettes. I mean I *love* smoking but I *hate* what it might do to me.
i Cigarettes do not tempt me in the slightest. They never have. And I *can't stand* being in public places which are full of smokers.

📖**4** Put the italicized verbs from the comments in exercise 3 into the table below.

Words connected with liking	Words connected with disliking

📖**5** Put these words in the correct place in the chart in exercise 4.

> *revolting be fond of charming be devoted to detestable loveable adorable enchanting captivating tempting enticing to fancy hateful odious disgusting desirable repulsive*

ACTIVATE

6 Use expressions from exercise 5 to say how you feel about the following.

a politicians
b dogs
c modern architecture
d personal stereos
e clothes (say which type you are talking about)

WORD FORMATION

PARTS OF SPEECH
Part A   Unit 7

7 Complete the chart.

Adjective	Noun	Verb
revolting		
charming		
		devote
loveable		
adorable		
enchanting		
captivating		
tempting		
enticing		
fanciable		fancy
hateful		
disgusting		
desirable		
repulsive		

8 Complete the blanks with the correct form of the word in brackets.

a Heavy drinking is really (harm) _____ to the liver.

b The sight of someone who has had too much to drink is really (disgust) _____.

c Some people are (captivate) _____ by the confidence of people who have had a drink or two.

d Most of us, however, tend to (repulse) _____ the advances of inebriated people.

e Once you have had a drink there is a strong (tempt) _____ to have another.

f People who have had a lot to drink often find members of the opposite sex more (entice) _____ than they do when they are sober.

g There are two kinds of drinkers; those that are (love) _____ and that are (detest) _____.

h The main thing — if you want to drink — is not to become (addict) _____ to the stuff.

ACTIVATE

9 Make statements about the following using words from exercise 8.

a football hooligans
b grandmothers
c pornography
d drugs
e ballet dancers

WORD GRAMMAR

VERB COMPLEMENTATION
Part A   Unit 12

10 Are the following verbs followed by *to* + infinitive or by an -*ing* verb? Tick the boxes.

Verb	-*ing* verb	*to* + infinitive
like		
love		
hate		
dislike		
detest		
enjoy		
loathe		
adore		
fond of		
can't stand		
(not) keen on		
don't care for		
be (really) into		

WORD USE

COLLOCATION
Part A   Unit 5

11 Match the sentences **a, b, c,** with their meanings **i, ii, iii.**

a I quite like champagne.
b I'm rather fond of champagne!
c I really like champagne.

i My feelings are a bit stronger than just liking.
ii I like it to a certain degree, but not that much.
iii I like it very much.

12 Say which of these sentences are correct and which don't sound right.

a I really hate driving in the rush hour.
b I'm absolutely keen on travelling by train.
c I absolutely love fast cars.
d I quite loathe flying.
e I simply adore expensive cars.
f I fairly detest travelling by bus.
g I really enjoy first class travel.

13 Based on the previous exercise, say which of the qualifying words on the left:

| absolutely fairly quite |
| rather really simply |

a are used with more neutral words
b are used with stronger words for liking and disliking
c can be used with either

Which cannot be used with verbs?

ACTIVATE

14 Use language from exercises 10–13 to agree and disagree. with these statements.

a 'I'm keen on Mozart myself.'
b 'I hate her dress, don't you?'
c 'He's a very selfish person. I don't like him at all.'
d 'I preferred her third husband. This one's incredibly stupid.'
e 'This meat is absolutely delicious. I just love beef.'
f 'God, I hate heavy metal music.'
g 'There's nothing I enjoy more than a night in a discotheque.'

WORD USE

METAPHOR AND IDIOM
Part A Unit 4

15 These people are talking about Ralph's music. Complete the chart with the name of the speakers.

Likes Ralph's music	Is neutral about Ralph's music	Doesn't like Ralph's music

ACTIVATE

16 Write dialogues in which you use expressions from exercise 10 about the following:

a classical music
b rock music
c the music of a particular composer
d the music of a particular pop/rock star

17 Individually, write down two pet hates (things that you really can't stand) and two wild enthusiasms (things you are crazy about). You can write about anything you like, but here are some suggestions.

sport animals entertainment and leisure families work

a In groups compare your pet hates and wild enthusiasms. Choose a list of ten (five of each).
b Put your ten items in the Topics column of this chart.
c Interview other people about their reactions to the topics and score their response from 0 (= very negative) to 5 (= very positive).

Example *How do you feel about people smoking in restaurants?*
I absolutely detest it! (Score = 0/1)

Topics	Score					
1 _____	0	1	2	3	4	5
2 _____	0	1	2	3	4	5
3 _____	0	1	2	3	4	5
4 _____	0	1	2	3	4	5
5 _____	0	1	2	3	4	5
6 _____	0	1	2	3	4	5
7 _____	0	1	2	3	4	5
8 _____	0	1	2	3	4	5
9 _____	0	1	2	3	4	5
10 _____	0	1	2	3	4	5

d Take the total score for each topic and then divide it by the number of people you interviewed. Use the result to make statements to the rest of the class.

FOCUS WORDS
LIKES AND DISLIKES

absolutely	detestable	fairly	quite
addict	devote	fanciable	odious
admirer	disgust	fancy (v)	prefer
adorable	disgusting	harm	rather
adore (v)	dislike (v)	hate (v)	really
can't stand	distasteful	hateful	repulse
captivate	enchanting	like (v)	repulsive
captivating	entice	likeable	revolting
charming	enticing	loathe (v)	simply
delicious	enjoy	love (v)	tempt
desirable	enjoyable	loveable	tempting
detest (v)			

FOCUS PHRASES

be a fan of	I don't (really) care for
be an aficionado	I don't (really) care for
be devoted to	I'm not (really) bothered
be fond of	(it) leaves me cold
be (not) keen on	(it's) not up to much
be (really) into	(it's) out of this world
get a kick out of	(it really) turns me on
(it really) gets on my nerves	pet hate

1 Which of the following statements do you agree with? Why? Mark each sentence from 0 to 3 (0 = disagree, 3 = agree strongly). Then compare your answers with a partner's.

a The character differences between different nationalities can help cause wars.
b In any nation, the same variety of character types is represented.
c There's no such thing as 'national character'.

2 Which factor do you think most influences national character (if you believe there is such a thing)?
☐ climate ☐ history ☐ food
☐ geography (mountain, desert, jungle, etc.)
☐ other (please specify)? _____.

3 Read the following text quickly to find out what the author feels about the following.

a Americans as tourists.
b The way others describe American tourists.

The ways of tourists are strange, and one afternoon as I sat in the Plaza Mayor, I heard some Frenchmen at the next table tearing Americans apart. To the first barrage of criticism, I could not logically protest: Americans were uncultured, lacked historical sense, were concerned only with business, had no sensitivity and ought to stay at home. The second echelon of abuse I did want to interrupt, because I felt that some of it was wide of the mark: Americans were all loud, had no manners, no education no sense of proportion, and were offensively vulgar in dress, speech, eating habits and general comportment, but I restrained myself because, after all, this was a litany one heard throughout Europe, here expressed rather more succinctly than elsewhere.

Sitting as quietly as my French companions would permit, I tried to discover what my true feelings were in this matter of honest description. In my travels, I had never met any single Americans as noisy and crude as certain Germans, none so downright mean as one or two Frenchmen, none so ridiculous as an occasional Englishman, and none so arrogant as some Swedes.

But in each of the national examples cited I am speaking only of a few horrible specimens. If one compares all English tourists with all Americans, I would have to admit that taken in the large the American is worse. If some European wanted to argue that seventy percent of all American tourists are regrettable, I would agree. If he claimed ninety, I suppose I wouldn't argue too much. But when like the Frenchman on my left he states that one hundred percent are that way, then I must accuse him of being false to the facts.

James Michener *Iberia 2*

4 Discuss these questions with a partner.

a What nationality do you think the author is? Why?
b Have you ever seen American tourists visiting a place? If so, do you agree with the Frenchman's opinion?
c What does the author dislike most about the way people talk about other nationalities?
d What does the author seem to think about the concept of 'national character'?

MEANING

SENSE RELATIONS
Part A   Unit 3

---

5 a Find words or phrases in the passage with opposite meanings to the following.

> *cultivated   sensitive   good-mannered   quiet   refined generous   modest   admirable*

b Which nationality is each of the words you have found used to describe?
c Here are some other words commonly associated with certain nationalities. From the list below find as many pairs of opposites as possible.

> *reserved   lively   talkative   polite   aggressive   boring hard-working   inflexible   lazy   inscrutable   cheerful frank   hypocritical   genuine   eccentric   fun well-organized   male-chauvinist   flamboyant   unpunctual*

ACTIVATE

6 a How would you describe the typical characteristics of your own nationality?
b Match these nationalities with the 'stereotype' pictures.

> *the French   the Russians   the Japanese   the Brazilians the Americans   the Chinese   the Swiss   the British*

Are the stereotypes fair? Describe the stereotypical character of two or three different nationalities.

MEANING

CONNOTATION
Part A   Unit 3

📖**7** The following are all nouns. Which are negative or 'bad' characteristics, which are positive or 'good' characteristics, and which could be either positive or negative depending on the circumstances? Use a dictionary to help you decide.

> *mischievousness   playfulness   evil   patience   ferocity   grace
> stupidity   serenity   pride   vanity   cunning   greed
> gentleness   loyalty   deceit   bravery   obstinacy
> independence   cleverness   cowardice   modesty*

Positive	Negative	Positive or negative

WORD FORMATION
NOUNS AND ADJECTIVES
Part A   Unit 7

8 Find adjectives to complete the following dialogues. Each adjective should relate to one of the nouns in exercise 7.

a MANAGER: I find it very hard to persuade my new assistant to work in the way I want her to. She's very _____.

b YOUNG ACTOR: George is extremely proud of his good looks and constantly looks at himself in the mirror.
OTHER YOUNG ACTOR: Yes, he's really _____.

c CRITIC: That writer is far too _____.
PUBLISHER: Yes, she will never admit how good her work is.

d SMALL GIRL: They're wonderful dancers, aren't they? They move so beautifully.
FATHER: Yes, they're really _____.

e UNCLE: Your children can be very _____. Yesterday they put a banana skin outside my bedroom door.
MOTHER: Did you hurt yourself?

f TRAIN DRIVER: The passengers have been waiting for hours and hours without complaining.
GUARD: Yes, it's hard to understand how people can be so _____ when the service we run is so terrible.

g TEACHER: Linda was very _____: she managed to avoid doing her homework by saying that she had to visit her boyfriend in hospital.
OTHER TEACHER: It's probably true. He broke his leg yesterday.

h MARY: Although his wife has left him several times for other men, Ben has always remained _____ to her and has never had a close relationship with another woman.
JULIE: Really? What were you doing coming out of the disco with him last night, then?

9 a What is your favourite animal? Why? Compare your answer with a partner's.
b Which animal(s) would you associate with each of the characteristics listed in exercises 7 and 8? Are any of the qualities associated *only* with human beings?

MEANING

RELATED AND UNRELATED
MEANING
Part A   Unit 2

📖**10** Put the words below into the appropriate columns in the table.

> snobbish   barbarous   impartial   heroic   affectionate
> diligent   arrogant   objective   devoted   overbearing
> sadistic   fearless   courageous   conscientious   fair
> industrious   conceited   long-suffering

boastful	tolerant	loving	violent	brave	hard-working

In each column, add one or two famous people from history (especially the history of your country) who you think had/have the characteristics listed.

MEANING

METAPHOR
Part A   Unit 4

11 These people are all talking about other people's characters. Match the names they mention with the descriptions in the box.

a *someone you can really rely on*
b *someone who is very concerned for and generous to others*
c *someone with a lot of energy and enthusiasm*
d *someone with a very high opinion of himself/herself*
e *someone who talks too much*
f *someone who is very quiet but seems sure of himself/herself*
g *someone who is very timid*
h *someone who loses his/her temper quickly*

ACTIVATE

12 Look at these photos. What can you tell from them about the character of each person? (Use phrases like: *He looks... /I would guess she's a_____ person/ To judge from appearances, he's...*, etc.)

Which of these people would you:

a not like to have an argument with.
b like to go on holiday with.
c like to have with you in an emergency.
d not want to have as a houseguest.

Give reasons for your decisions.

FOCUS WORDS

CHARACTER AND
PERSONALITY 1

admirable	diligent	independent	polite
affectionate	disorganized	independence	impolite
aggressive	eccentric	industrious	proud
arrogant	evil	inflexible	pride
barbarous	fair	inscrutable	punctual
boastful	fearless	lazy	quiet
big-head	ferocious	lively	refined
big-headed	ferocity	long-suffering	reserved
boring	flamboyant	loyal	sadistic
brave	flexible	loyalty	sensitive
bravery	inflexible	male-chauvinist	sensitivity
chatterbox	frank	manners	serene
cheerful	fun	mean	serenity
clever	generous	mischievous	snobbish
cleverness	gentle	mischievousness	stupid
conceited	gentleness	modest	stupidity
conscientious	genuine	modesty	talkative
cowardly	good-	noisy	tolerant
cowardice	mannered	objective	uncultured
courageous	graceful	obstinate	unpunctual
crude	grace	obstinacy	vain
cultivated	greedy	overbearing	vanity
cultured	greed	patient	violent
cunning	hard-working	patience	vulgar
deceitful	heroic	playful	warm-hearted
deceit	hypocritical	playfulness	well-organized
devoted	impartial		

FOCUS PHRASES

be a ball of fire
be a tower of strength
fly off the handle

frightened of your own
　shadow
have no sense of proportion
the strong, silent type

16 *Character and personality 2*

1 How do you see yourself? Think about your own character and personality. Do you have any particular weaknesses or strengths? Write down three things which you think are good about your character and three things which you think are not so good. Then compare your list with a partner's.

2 Read these brief character descriptions. Can you match the photos to the descriptions? Which of these four people sounds most like you? Which would you most like to meet?

Amrita

'I'm an active and energetic person – I can't bear just sitting around doing nothing. It just makes me impatient and restless. But I know what I want, and I think I've got what it takes to achieve my goals. Does that make me sound horribly ambitious and selfish? I hope not!'

Kevin

'I'm the kind of person who knows how to have a good time. I suppose you would call me fun-loving, but it's more than that. I actually believe in a calm, cool, easy-going approach to life and I can't bear unnecessary anxiety and pressure. I believe in being sociable and taking life as it comes . . .'

Larry

'My problem can be summarized in one word: self-confidence. I just don't have enough. I'm shy with other people, who must think I'm boring and stupid sometimes. Lack of confidence also makes me indecisive: I spend days trying to make up my mind what to do about quite simple things. I'm told I sometimes look moody, but in fact I like being with other people . . .'

Cathy

'How do I see myself? Well, I'm forgetful and disorganized – some would say absent-minded! But I've got quite a lot of willpower, really, and I've got ideas. I'm a hardworker too when I'm doing something I'm interested in. I'm not very articulate when it comes to public speaking but I quite enjoy being the centre of attention, and I don't get in the least bit nervous.'

MEANING

CONNOTATION
Part A   Unit 3

3 The words below are taken from the character descriptions. Which describe positive qualities, which describe negative qualities, and which describe qualities which could be positive *or* negative (neutral)?

> impatient   active   energetic   restless   ambitious   selfish
> fun-loving   calm   cool   easy-going   sociable   stupid
> indecisive   shy   boring   moody   forgetful   disorganized
> nervous   absent-minded   articulate   anxiety   willpower
> hard worker   self-confidence

Positive	Negative	Neutral

WORD FORMATION

ADJECTIVES AND NOUNS
Part A   Unit 7

4 Find nouns to correspond to as many of the adjectives above as possible. Use the endings *-sion/-tion, -ness, -ence,* etc.

MEANING

RELATED AND UNRELATED
MEANINGS
Part A   Unit 2

5 Match these adjectives with opposites from the list in exercise 3 above. Then try to find opposites for the others in the list (some are in the list itself).

> lethargic   confident   clever   magnanimous   excitable   lazy

ACTIVATE

6 a Choose three adjectives from exercises 3 and 5 to describe your own character. At least one of the adjectives must be negative, and at least one must be positive. Tell a partner about your character and see if they agree.
  b Write a brief (50–100 word) description of the character of your ideal partner. Use words from the lists above and others like the following.

> modest/proud/vain   creative/artistic   eccentric
> narrow-minded/broad-minded   kind/considerate   cautious

Exchange descriptions with your neighbour and talk about the differences.

7 Read this description of a famous 18th century British writer, who was one of the first to write about women's rights. As you read, try to answer the following questions.

a What kind of person was she?
b Would you have admired her if you had met her? Why/Why not?

A harsh and unhappy childhood, dominated by an unstable and drunken father whom she never respected, gave Mary Wollstonecraft an unusual sense of her own independence and reliance on her own judgement; and a corresponding lack of respect for all kinds of male authority that she did not feel had been genuinely earned, whether in life or in literature. At the same time this passionate, ebullient and frequently opinionated woman was given to terrible swings of mood, from hectic, noisy enthusiasm to almost suicidal depression and a sense of futility and loneliness.
Richard Holmes *Footsteps*

8 List the words and phrases in the text that describe Mary Wollstonecraft. Which of these words and phrases imply that the author approves of her character, and which may indicate weaknesses?

WORD FORMATION

WORD USE
Part A   Unit 7

9 The adjectives and nouns in the table all have to do with character and personality. Complete the table by finding nouns corresponding to the adjectives and adjectives corresponding to the nouns.

Adjectives	Nouns	Adjectives	Nouns
moody	mood	carefree	xxxxx
emotional		warm-hearted	
	despair		vivacity
likeable	xxxxx		liveliness
prejudiced		anxious	
	affection		enthusiasm
passionate		independent	
	charm		instability
optimistic		domineering	xxxxx
	pessimism	lonely	

Do the adjectives and nouns describe an attitude to other people, an attitude to life in general or both?

ACTIVATE

10 Complete the passage with appropriate words from this unit.

My uncle Desmond is the kind of person everyone likes. In fact, he's so a) _____ that neighbours and friends visit him constantly. Luckily, he enjoys other people's company.

Almost everyone finds Desmond charming, and as far as I can tell his b) _____ lies in the fact that he always takes a positive view of life. In fact, many people find his c) _____ infectious. I've seen people who are really d) _____ suddenly forget all their terrible worries and become full of life. Last week one woman became so e) _____ that she started dancing on the table, which amused Desmond.

Another thing I like about Desmond is that he is very broad-minded about everything from religion through food to nationality. I have rarely met anyone with so few f) _____ and so much g) _____ for life.

Not surprisingly, although Desmond lives alone, he always has company, so he never feels h) _____ . On the other hand, he doesn't seem to need the help of anyone, in spite of being over 80, and lives a very i) _____ life.

11 In this dialogue, B's responses have become mixed up. Indicate their correct position by putting a number in the brackets (the first one has been done for you).

A: So that's your friend, Damien
B: [1] I've known him for ages. We used to go to school together.
A: What's he like?
B: [ ] Well . . . perhaps I'd better introduce him to you . . .
A: I thought you said he <u>has a tendency</u> to be aggressive.
B: [ ] Aristocratic? Damien? Maybe he <u>gives that impression</u> . . . yes, now you mention it, he does <u>have an arrogant streak</u>.
A: <u>There's a touch of the aristocratic about him</u>, I find . . .
B: [ ] Yes, I think <u>he takes after</u> his father, who was <u>well-known for</u> his bad temper.
A: I don't mean that exactly. I think <u>there's something</u> quite distinguished <u>about him</u>.
B: [ ] He's <u>the quiet type</u>, but he's <u>not as shy as he seems</u> . . . I'm quite fond of him.
A: Oh, yes please!

12 Use the underlined expressions from exercise 11 to describe someone in your family or one of your friends to a partner.

ACTIVATE

13 What were you like at age 12? What do you think you will be like at age 70? Write brief descriptions of yourself at these two ages.

FOCUS WORDS
CHARACTER AND PERSONALITY 2

absent-minded	despair	independent	pessimistic
active	desperate	instability	phlegmatic
affection	disorganized	kind	prejudice
affectionate	domineering	lazy	prejudiced
ambitious	easy-going	lethargic	pressure
anxious	ebullient	likeable	proud
anxiety	eccentric	lively	restless
articulate	emotion	liveliness	restlessness
artistic	emotional	lonely	self-confident
boring	energetic	loneliness	self-confidence
broad-minded	enthusiasm	modest	selfish
calm	enthusiastic	moody	shy
care	excitable	narrow-minded	sociable
carefree	forgetful	nervous	stable
cautious	fun-loving	opinionated	stupid
charm	hardworking	optimism	unambitious
charming	hard worker	optimistic	unstable
cheerful	impatience	organized	vain
confused	impatient	passion	vivacity
considerate	inarticulate	passionate	vivacious
cool	indecisive	patient	warm-hearted
creative	independence	pessimism	willpower
decisive			

FOCUS PHRASES

be the centre of attention
be the _____ kind/type
(I) can't bear
(I've) got what it takes (to)
have a _____ streak
have a tendency to
lack confidence
lack of respect (for)
make up (my) mind

not as _____ as he/she
  seems
take after someone
take life as it comes
there's something _____
  about him/her
there's a touch of the
  _____ about him/her

PART A Key

UNIT 1
MEANING IN CONTEXT

Ex 1

trust = have confidence in someone or something
being single = not being married
galleries = museums of art
biographer = person who writes a biography or
  true life story

Ex 2

Open exercise

Ex 3

a she suddenly realized that she dealt almost
   exclusively with women rather than with both
   men and women
b she was writing a book about Lorin Jones; they
   grew up in the same area

Ex 4

Open exercise
[the text comes from literary fiction which is
humorous in parts]

Ex 5

Open exercise

Ex 6

therapist = someone who treats illnesses of the
  mind without using drugs
looked forward to = waited for with pleasure/
  expectation
rage = extreme anger
neighbouring = geographically next to
toddler = young child who has just learnt to walk

Ex 7

The original words were:
dealings, miserable, disasters, unknown, paths

Ex 8, 9

Open exercises

UNIT 2
RELATED AND UNRELATED MEANINGS

Ex 1

Some of the different meanings are
can = (verb) describing ability, permission,
         possibility etc
         (noun & verb) describing a tin container
book = (noun) something you read
         (verb) to reserve
         (verb) to have a crime recorded (to be
         "booked for speeding")
flat = (adjective) not pointed or bumpy
         (adjective) not fizzy (for drinks)
         (noun) an apartment
         (noun) short for a flat tyre
right = (adjective) opposite to left
         (adjective) opposite of wrong
         (noun) something given to you by law
         (adjective) "I agree"
left = (adjective) opposite of right
         (noun) people with left-wing convictions
         (past participle) from the verb "leave"
line = (noun) something between two points
         (noun) an utterance in a play
like = (verb) the opposite of dislike
         (adverb) "the same as"

Ex 2

Open exercise (this passage and the one that
follows it come from **The Man who Mistook his Wife for
a Hat** by Oliver Sacks in which the author describes
his work as a psychiatrist)

Ex 3

a (suggested answer) the man was perfectly
   normal when he came in, but seemed to be very
   excited and strange later.
b Open exercise

Ex 4

Some alternative meanings for the words are:

singular = opposite of plural
patient = calm, prepared to wait
admitted = finally say that you did something
  wrong
second = a sixtieth of a minute
carrying on = continuing
floor = level of a building (noun) or to knock
  someone over (verb)

Ex 5

a admitted   floor   second   c patient
b singular   singular   d seconds

Ex 6

(suggested answers)
a The waiter drops the tray
b Raindrops keep falling on my head!
c Aircraft drop supplies
d Lineker has been dropped from the team
e Careful! There's a steep drop of at least 1,000
  feet

Ex 7

(suggested answers)
a someone with an illness lies down
  someone who is being interviewed by the police
  lies (= doesn't tell the truth)
b someone in a classroom makes a row (= noise)
  someone in a boat rows, using two oars
c someone at a party makes a terrible racket
  (= noise)
  someone playing tennis or squash uses a racket
  a criminal might well be involved in a racket
  where stolen cars are sold as new
d you use glue to stick a model of a car together
  an old person going for a walk uses a (walking-)
  stick
e people in restaurants give waiters tips
  when you ask for advice you may ask for a few
  'tips'
  I can't quite remember the word even though it's
  on the tip of my tongue
  she tipped her drink right down the front of my
  shirt

Ex 8

Open exercise

Ex 9

The suggested groups are:
a amusement, joke, sense of humour
b patient, test, neurologist, dissect
c fall asleep, wake up, bedclothes

Ex 10

a alarm, bewilderment, consternation, stunned,
  amazement, incredible.
b anger, horrible, disgust

Ex 11

Open exercise

Ex 12

Least .... annoyed .... angry .... furious .... **Most**

Ex 13, 14

Open exercises

UNIT 3
SENSE RELATIONS

Ex 1

Most general	More specific	Most specific
a) cooking	boil	simmer
b) animals	bear	polar bear
c) drink	beer	lager
d) goes	walking	strolling

Ex 2

a driver, man, forty-five-year-old father of two
b delivery van, vehicle, Ford Transit
c severely damaged, windscreen smashed, a
  virtual write-off

Ex 3

customer – 20-year-old bank clerk
proprietor – woman
customer – young man
proprietor – apologetic Mrs Castro

Ex 4

(suggested answers)
cat, rescued, Siamese, owner, save, pet, university
professor, mother of six, animal lover, bring the
exhausted animal to safety

Ex 5

(suggested answers)
a reptile – crocodile, lion – lion cub etc.
b thief, burglar, drug pusher, murderer etc.
c high-rise development, block of flats etc.

Ex 6

Open exercise

Ex 7

(suggested answers)

a exhausted
b terrible/dreadful
c an idiot
d thrilled/delighted
e demolished/flattened
f fall asleep

Ex 8

(suggested answers – the opposites will depend on the exact sense in which you are using the original word)

strong – weak, *evil* – good, *ancient* – modern, *patient* – impatient, *broad* – narrow, *optimistic* – pessimistic, *luxurious* – squalid, *impetuous* – careful, *exciting* – boring, *cool* – warm

Ex 9

(suggested answers)

blow hot and cold – someone who keeps changing their opinion (being very enthusiastic about an idea one minute and completely against it the next). *"I don't understand why you keep blowing hot and cold over this."*

in black and white – making something crystal clear. *"Why can't you understand it? Must I spell it out in black and white?"*

the long and the short of it – the general conclusion of a situation or story without going into any more detail. *"So the long and short of it is I've lost my job."*

off and on – occasionally, from time to time. *"Are you attending those viola lessons?" "Yeah, sort of off and on."*

a love-hate relationship – when you have conflicting emotions about a thing or person and you (probably) can't tear yourself away. *"I have a love-hate relationship with Mexico City. I mean the atmosphere's fantastic, but the traffic and the pollution..."*

back and forth – something moves from one extreme to the other. *In the board room the argument went back and forth for hours.*

UNIT 4
METAPHOR, IDIOMS, PROVERBS

Ex 1

a roar
b hoot
c purr
d cackle, squawk
e bark
f squawk
g grunt
h whinny
i bleat

Ex 2

Open exercise

Ex 3

(suggested answers)

"Get your hair cut," he roared/barked
"Get out of my house and don't come back," he roared/barked
"Ooh that's funny," she hooted
"A ghost? In my house? Eeeek!" he squawked
"Hmmph! The country's going to the dogs," she grunted
"Another one for the basket," she cackled
"But I don't want to," he bleated
"I like it when you bring me presents," she purred

Ex 4

verbs that can be used:

a bark, roar
b cackle
c bleat, squawk
d whinny, grunt, hoot etc
e roar

Ex 5

a it rained very heavily
b when they woke up snow was covering the whole landscape
c the wind made a noise in the trees like someone letting out a deep breath

Ex 6

a the feeling someone has when standing in a very strong (probably tropical) wind: a storm
b some sort of fierce animal, like a dragon or a tiger

Ex 7

a the wind *clawed*...
b *scratched* and *bit*...

c *roared with rage*...
d *steam of hot breath*...
e *growling, loose-limbed*
f *sting of its tail*
g ...towards some other *prey*

Ex 8

a let sleeping dogs lie
b I may as well be hanged for a sheep as for a lamb
c straight from the horse's mouth
d flog a dead horse
e put the cat among the pigeons
f the lion's share
g play cat and mouse
h sort out the sheep from the goats

Ex 9

a flog (horse)
b hang (sheep)
c cat
d dog

Ex 10

a right
b wrong – should be 'hold your horses'
c wrong – should be 'male chauvinist pig'
d wrong – should be 'kill two birds with one stone'
e right

Ex 11

(possible answers)
a 'She was riding her bike. Suddenly it started to rain cats and dogs, so...'
b 'He told her about..., which really set the cat among the pigeons'
c 'When George realized the company had found him out, he decided that he might as well be hanged for a sheep as for a lamb'
d 'Mary refused to let sleeping dogs lie and campaigned to get her neighbours to help to clean up the area...'
e 'While they were in town, Pat and Dave decided to kill two birds with one stone: first they...; then they...'

Ex 12

a It's better to sort out problems while it's easy to do so. Otherwise it could be a lot harder

b Even if you have doubts about someone, you will have even more doubts about somebody else who you don't know at all
c Don't depend completely on one thing
d If you do something wrong to someone who has done wrong to you, that won't make things right
e It's better to hold on to something you're sure of than to take a risk in order to get something which seems better
f In order to have an agreement, you need two people to say 'yes'

Ex 13

Open exercise

UNIT 5
COLLOCATION – WHICH WORD GOES WITH WHICH?

Ex 1

drive a bus, ride this bicycle, nod your head, shrug your shoulders, tell a lie, say a word in Russian, make your bed, do your homework

drive: a car, a lorry, a hard bargain, me crazy
tell: your father, a story, a lie
say: nothing, something, yes
make: a mistake, a cake, money
do: the washing up, a job, damage

Ex 2

(suggested answers)
a 'fat' is unusual with 'wood': we say a 'thick piece of wood'
b right
c right
d we don't use 'dead' with 'apple': we say a 'rotten apple'
e right
f wrong: we say a 'silly mistake', a 'stupid mistake', a 'serious mistake' etc
g right
h drinks aren't 'heavy' (although drinkers are): we say a 'strong drink'.
i we don't use 'touching' in this way: we can say a 'helping hand'
j right

heavy: drinker, conversation
strong: opinion, medicine
fat: cheque, profit
thick: fog, ear

Ex 3
Open exercise

Ex 4
interested in music, enthusiastic about the game, different from the bread we eat, keen on learning Spanish, late for her appointment with the doctor, afraid of large dogs, polite to his boss, disgusted with me

(suggested answers)
about: crazy about jazz, optimistic about the results
for: eager for praise, desperate for money
with: paralyzed with fear, pleased with her progress
of: scared of heights, typical of his behaviour

Ex 5
launched, raise, limit, by, consumption, heavy, rate, to, diet, intake
to launch a campaign
to limit a disease/epidemic
to reduce alcohol consumption
to raise awareness
it was agreed by them
heavy drinking/smoking
the death/birth rate is high
a rich diet of fatty foods/sugar
avoid exposure to the sun
a healthy diet

Ex 6, 7
Open exercises

Ex 8

	a story	something	in a quiet voice	a lie	French	yes or no	the truth
speak			✓		✓		✓
say		✓				✓	
tell	✓			✓			✓

Ex 9
a The tall man in the blue jacket was telling the truth when he said this city was popular with tourists
b Last night Jim told his little daughter a story about a prince who was kidnapped by a very tall giant
c There were only four or five journalists present, but the Prime Minister spoke in a loud voice, as if she was addressing them from a high balcony
d Julia speaks quite good Spanish and Portuguese
e He never remembers to say 'please' and 'thank you'

Ex 10
Open exercise

UNIT 6
STYLE AND REGISTER

Ex 1
Conversation 1:
I'm sorry to bother you, but do you mind my asking where you bought that charming bag?
— Not at all. As a matter of fact it was a present from a friend in India
Really? Could I possibly have a closer look?
— Certainly. As you can see it's handmade.
It's absolutely exquisite. Thank you so much for showing it to me

Conversation 2:
Hey I love your coat. Where did you get it?
— It's my sister's. Nice, isn't it?
Can I have a proper look?
— Hang on . . . here you are. Hand-made you know
Thanks. Wow, it's great! I don't suppose you.
know where she got it?
— No, sorry.

The difference between the conversations is that (1) is fairly formal whereas (2) is fairly informal.

Ex 2
(suggested answers)
a 1 b 2 c 3 d 2 e 3 (e.g. difference between private conversations and talking to a large audience.)

Answer key 165

Ex 3
a formal
b informal
c formal
d informal
e formal

Ex 4
Open exercise

Ex 5
a this letter is formal ('in the course of the week...', 'sorriest victims', 'announcements were made to the effect...')
b this letter is neutral
c this letter is informal (use of 'bloody', 'take the biscuit', very direct questions, e.g. 'Do you honestly think...')

Ex 6
Dear Sir (F), twice (N), roll up to work (I), regular passenger (N), to the effect that (F), the fifth time I've written (N), take the biscuit (I), didn't even bother (I), I can tell you (I), at your hands (F), the sorriest victims (F), cancelled (N), please suggest (F), bloody trains (I), maybe (I), enclosing (N), just ended (N), overpriced (N), due to (N)

Ex 7
Open exercise

Ex 8

Informal/Colloquial	Neutral	Formal
copper/ the old Bill dough/dosh/bread pad boss	policeman money home superior get	dwelling obtain

Ex 9
Open exercise

Ex 10
a On a (merchant) navy ship. Sailor and captain
b In a church or registry office. Priest/official and bride
c In a car. Driving instructor and pupil
d In somebody's house. Carpenter/builder and house owner

Ex 11
(suggested answers)
a thing/tool for putting in screws
a machine for mixing foods
a vehicle for carrying dead people
a building in which soldiers live
a person who gets coal from the ground

Ex 12, 13
Open exercises

UNIT 7
PARTS OF SPEECH: VERBS AND NOUNS

Ex 1
1 e 2 f 3 g 4 b 5 c 6 h 7 a 8 i 9 d

Ex 2
Open exercise

Ex 3
I hid (V) in a (D) half-finished building (N). It was made of red (Adj) brick (N) but had no roof. Trees and (C) grass as high (Adj) as the walls of the house had grown inside (Adv). I went through (P) a window frame so as not to leave (V) any marks around (P) the door, and hid fearfully (Adv) in the grass. I tried to keep quiet (Adj). I tried not to think of (P) the snakes that were probably (Adv) around me.

Ex 4

Infinitive	Present part.	Past	Past part.
hide	hiding	hid	hidden
make	making	made	made
have	having	had	had
grow	growing	grew	grown
go	going	went	gone
leave	leaving	left	left
try	trying	tried	tried
keep	keeping	kept	kept
think	thinking	thought	thought

The difference is that all these verbs are irregular

Ex 5
trees — tree; walls — wall; marks — mark; snakes — snake

Ex 6
a donkeys
b tomatoes
c oxen
d mice
e mouse traps
f pianos
g pheasants
h fish
i cloths
j syllabuses/syllabi
k ships
l stars
m elephants
n men
o skies
p ostriches
q cellos
r symphonies

Ex 7
a Open exercise
b He has children, so he's not that young; he likes cold beer and buttered toast; he is trying to escape; he is concerned for his friend/friends

Ex 8
He's in a building which hasn't been finished and has no roof or windows. It's a tropical area because there are tropical snakes there, and there are trees and long grass around the building and inside it.

Ex 9, 10, 11
Open exercises

UNIT 8
AFFIXES

Ex 1
noun – singular: —ment
noun – plural: —ren
verbs: —ed, —ing
adjectives: —ant, —ed, —able, —ous, —ive

Ex 2

Noun	Adjective	Adverb	Verb
quickness	quick	quickly	quicken
simplification	simple	simply	simplify
legality	legal	legally	legalize
dirt	dirty	dirtily	dirty
painlessness	painless	painlessly	pain*
hope	hopeful	hopefully	hope
drive, driving	driving		drive
stupidity	stupid	stupidly	stupefy
retirement	retired/retiring*	retiringly*	retire
washing, wash	washable		wash

a -en; -ify; -ize; -y
b -ness; - (ifica)tion; -ity; -ment
c -y; -less; -ful; -ed; - ing

*Note that:
a) The verb 'to pain' is quite rare, and often only used in set phrases. e.g. 'It pains me dreadfully to have to give you such bad news'.
b) Although 'retire' means 'to stop working', the adjective 'retiring' also has a secondary meaning; 'shy and reserved', and the adverb 'retiringly' has *only* this second meaning.

Ex 3
a not
b not
c not
d not
e down
f not
g not
h out
i too much
j before
k from
l together
m again
n after

possible without prefixes: approve, expensive, happy, legal, sense, possible, estimate, arrange

not possible without prefixes: descend, expel, predict, subtract, coincide, postpone

Ex 4
a unkind
b illiterate
c intemperate
d dishonest
e decentralize
f irregular
g non-resident
h impolite

Ex 5
1 anxiety
2 unwell
9 hysterical
10 implication

3 disagreeable
4 yelled
5 underestimated
6 actively
7 discovery
8 literally
11 amazement
12 cruelty
13 decision
14 considerably
15 dangerous

Ex 6
Open exercise

Ex 7
I can't stay here anymore because of Miss Turner.

UNIT 9
SPELLING AND SOUNDS

Ex 1
a same **b** same **c** different **d** same

Ex 2
all are different

Ex 3
a hopping/hopped
b hoping/hoped
c fatter/fattest
d later/latest
e phoning /phoned
f faster/fastest
g beating
h developing/developed
i beginning
j rebelling/rebelled
k excelling/excelled
l referring/referred
m opening/opened
n visiting/visited
o panicking/panicked
p picnicking/picnicked
q batting/batted
r marshalling/marshalled
s omitting/omitted
t bleating/bleated

Ex 4
a the final consonant doubles
b nothing changes
c nothing changes
d nothing changes
e the final consonant doubles
f the final consonant doubles
g k is added after the c

Ex 5
When the final -e would be followed by a vowel it is deleted

If the word ends in -ee the final e remains
If the word ends in -ge or -ce the final e remains
When the final -e is followed by a consonant, it remains
The three words in (e) are exceptions

Ex 6
a c **b** w **c** c **d** w **e** c **f** c **g** c **h** w

Except in the case of 'friend', *ei* or *ie* are being used to represent a long /i : / sound.

'Seize' is an exception because the rule is that *i* should come before *e* except when the letter before *i* is c.

Ex 7
a A **b** A/B **c** B **d** B **e** A **f** B **g** B **h** A
i B **j** A **k** A **l** B

Ex 8
I love my daddy because he gives me a good education.
My mummy says I must love everybody, even the people who killed my daddy, but I don't.
My dad went to prison and we have to keep remembering to love him.
My teacher is very cruel. She smacks people all day and she eats frogs' legs and makes cross spells. I don't like her because she says I tell fibs.
My father has a cross face in the holidays.
Old ladies aren't really old ladies. They're just people wearing old clothes.

Ex 9, 10
Open exercises

UNIT 10
COUNTABLE AND UNCOUNTABLE

Ex 1
milk (B), medicine (B), new shirt (A), day off (A), chewing tobacco (B), companionship (B), meal in a restaurant (A), pair of scissors (A), banana (A), ticket (A), biscuit (A), brown sugar (B), mineral water (A/B), ride on my motorbike (A), friendly advice (B), useful information (B), money (B), help (B), salt (B), work (B)

All the 'A's are countable; all the 'B's are uncountable.

Ex 2
Open exercise

Ex 3

Uncountable	Countable
meat	bean sprouts
garlic	mushrooms
oil	green pepper
sauce	noodles
pepper	onion

(suggested answers)
a a slice of bread, cheese, ham
b two spoonfuls of sugar, flour
c a loaf of bread
d a glass of orange juice, port, milk
e a piece of bread, cake, cheese
f a cup of coffee, tea, Bovril
g three bowls of soup, cornflakes, chilli con carne
h a bunch of grapes, bananas
i a pinch of salt, snuff, pepper
j a drop of lemon juice, oil

Ex 4
Open exercise

Ex 5
The nouns which should have ticks are:
light, mineral water, cauliflower, cola, ice cream, paper, lamb, salad, beauty, cake

The words that can only be used as uncountable nouns are:
courage, wood, homework, advice, information, anger, hope, smoking, weather

Ex 6
The incorrect sentences are:
d apple is countable so we don't say 'some apple'
e 'bread' is uncountable: we can't say 'breads'
f 'advice' is always uncountable; it can't be pluralized
g 'Dollars' is plural and refers to more than one dollar; we use 'many' with plural countables
i 'progress' is uncountable; it can't be pluralized

Ex 7
The nouns that only exist in a plural form are:
binoculars, shorts, clothes, scissors, earnings, people, premises, cattle, remains, (eye)glasses, thanks, outskirts

Ex 8
Open exercise

Ex 9
a Because my earnings have been dramatically affected by the rate of inflation.
b Your cattle are in my garden and they're eating my flowers and vegetables.
c I can assure you that the scales were checked and adjusted only last week.
d OK. The good news is that I passed my English exam; the bad news is that I was suspended for cheating.
e English people are usually shy and speak other languages badly.
f I think billiards is a much better game.
g My company's main premises are in London, but I usually work in Manchester. The premises in London house the Head Office and Sales Department.
h OK; where are the scissors? I haven't seen them for weeks.

Ex 10
Open exercise

UNIT 11
VERBS

Ex 1
a O b X c NO d X e NO f O g X
h X i NO j O

Ex 2
(suggested answers)
transitive: put, spill, entertain, take, tell, etc
intransitive: wander, cry, doze, gabble, hop, etc

Ex 3
(suggested answers)
a her boyfriend is overweight and doesn't like her

telling him about it. She's worried about his health
b she seems to be very fond of him
c because it may 'work wonders'

Ex 4
Open exercise

Ex 5
looks, try, feel

Ex 6
Open exercise

Ex 7
(suggested answers)
It describes a mother who is woken by her baby in the middle of the night (again)
It is both happy and sad (the mother and the baby are happy to comfort each other but the suggestion is that the mother is sad and needs that comfort)

Ex 8
Open exercise

Ex 9
(suggested answers)
get up = get out of bed
switch on = turn on
put on = clothes herself with
pick up = lifts the baby in her arms
turn down = refuse
put back = take the baby back to his cot

Ex 10
(suggested answers)
a *took off* = left the ground/started its journey
b *took off* = removed
c *looked it up* = searched the dictionary and found the word and the explanation of its meaning.
d *Come on* = hurry up!
e *gave them away* = handed them out to people as presents
f *put the meeting off* = postponed
g *broke down* = stopped working

Ex 11
The phrasal verbs in exercise 9 which are transitive are:
switch on, put on, pick up, turn down, put back.

The object comes after the particle with switch on and put on, but before the particle with pick up, turn down, put back.

Sometimes the particle (on, up, down, away etc) comes before the object. Sometimes it comes after the object. It always comes after an object which is a pronoun (it, him, her). If the object is a noun it can come before or after.

Ex 12
1 bringing them up
2 working out
3 split up
4 put Mike up in his flat
5 sent him away
6 rings them up
7 sets off
8 picks the children up
9 takes them out
10 warms up
11 take Alison and Peter back
12 gets up
13 invites the children out for lunch again

Ex 13
The prepositional verbs are: applied for, decided on, relying on, looking after

Ex 14
(suggested answers)
a I'm not going to tolerate your...
b Defend yourself, fight for yourself
c Try to reduce the amount...
d You must confront your problems/admit to your problems...

Ex 15
The corrections that should be made are:
b Get on with the story...
d Sue: No, I didn't make it up
f Get in the car
i I've thrown them away
j Get off my bicycle

Different meanings:
a Tidy up your clothes...
b Continue with the story...
c The plane left the ground...
d You invented that story...
e Can you give me a bed for the night?
f Enter the car...
g Remove the car from the garage...
h John's going to be Lyn's substitute...
i I've got rid of them
j Leave my bicycle/dismount from my bicycle

UNIT 12
VERB COMPLEMENTATION

Ex 1
(suggested answers)
a A charity asking for donations, especially legacies
b Some kind of massage machine, skin cream, slimming treatment etc.
c Holiday company, shipping line, travel agent
d Some kind of processed food, e.g. soup, dessert, sauce etc
e Medicine for a sore throat

Ex 2

Verb	Personal object	Other object
offering	you	a free 15 day trial
brings	to all the family	effective relief
leave	us	part of your estate
give	her family	something different
send	Beth Chapman	the coupon

Ex 3
(The answers are given in the text)

Ex 4

> Many verbs can be followed by a direct object + preposition + personal object.
> Some of these can be used in sentences with the pattern: verb + indirect object + direct object.
> It is necessary to learn which verbs can't take both patterns.
> When the direct object is a short prounoun (e.g. it, him), the indirect object will usually follow it.

Ex 5
a George read his children a story before they went to sleep
b Could you buy us a loaf of bread on your way home?
c Explain your joke to us
d I couldn't find Susie a clean pair of jeans
e Didn't you promise it to your mother-in-law
f The reporters asked the pop star so many questions that she got angry in the end
g Why don't you mention the pain to the doctor?
h Return the book to me as soon as you possibly can

i Why on earth did you lend Justin your motorbike?
j It was embarrassing. I had to borrow £10 from Ann

Ex 6
Open exercise

Ex 7
1 g 2 a 3 d 4 f 5 c 6 e 7 b 8 h

Ex 8
a 1 b 5 c 6 d 3 e 2 f 4 g 7 h 8

Ex 9
(suggested answers)
must: you must arrive on time, she must stop this game, I mustn't get into trouble again (a)
begin: he began to think about his future, she began to get tired of the conversation (b), he began driving even faster (d)
finish: she finished what she was doing (g), she finished typing the letter (d)
like: he likes to watch birds as they fly over (b), he doesn't like watching birds being shot (d), he likes eating pheasant (d)
hope: we hope to see you again soon (b), they hoped that they would be home before nightfall, she hoped that he would not ask her to marry him (f)
wonder: I wonder why he went away, he wondered whether it was going to rain, she wondered if she should tell him about the party (g)
make: she made me do it, I will make you laugh if it's the last thing I do (h)
ask: I'm not going to ask you again, he asked me to marry him (c), I asked her why she had not rung me earlier (g)
help: she helped them to see what the problem was (c), I'm going to help you play that piece one more time, will you help me try the lock again (h)
see: she saw me running down the street, I saw her laughing, we saw the plane circling overhead (d)
know: I don't know whether to believe you, I know what I think (g) how does she know that he's telling the truth? (f)

Ex 10
Open exercise

UNIT 1
THE HUMAN BODY

Ex 1

head	cheek eyebrow eyelid forehead lip mouth nose nostril
neck	Adam's apple
arm	armpit elbow forearm wrist
hand	little finger palm thumb wrist
upper torso	armpit back breast chest shoulder shoulder blades waist
lower torso	bottom hip navel small of the back stomach tummy waist
leg	ankle calf knee shin thigh
foot	ankle big toe heel little toe

Ex 2, 3
Open exercises

Ex 4
backache   tummy ache   stomach ache   headache

Ex 5
a He has a backache
b He has a stomach ache
c The woman has a headache
d She has a pain in her elbow
e The boy has hurt his knee
f The girl has earache
g He has a pain in his chest
h She has hurt her foot

Ex 6
(suggested answers)
a He's strained his back. He needs a rest/a massage
b He has indigestion. He should eat more slowly
c She is suffering from stress. She should take an aspirin
d She banged her elbow on something. She should have some heat treatment

e He twisted his knee playing football. He should wear an elastic bandage for a few days
f She may have an ear infection. She should see a doctor and get some ear drops
g He may have a heart condition. He should get a check-up/stop smoking etc.
h Her shoes were too tight. She could soak her foot in warm water

Ex 7
bones = hard parts which make up the 'frame' of the human or animal body. They're inside the flesh of your arms, legs, back, chest etc.
muscles = pieces of elastic material in the body which can be tightened to produce movements
blood = red liquid which flows through the body
lungs = the two 'bags' inside your chest that function as breathing organs
alimentary canal = the passage through which food passes in the body – made up of the oesophagus, the stomach, intestines etc.
kidneys = organs in the area of the lower back which separate waste liquid from blood
skin = the natural covering of animal and human bodies

Ex 8
there are 208 bones in the body
there are over 600 muscles, and these account for a lot of the body weight
in the blood system there are 5–6 litres of blood
our lungs breathe 500 cubic feet of air per day
our alimentary canal, which is about 25 feet long, has to deal with about 50 tons of food in our lives
our kidneys can deal with about 45 gallons of liquid a day
our skin measures about 17 square feet.

Ex 9
skeleton, muscles, blood system, heart, nervous system, lungs, 'cooling' system (sweat glands), feeding system, reproductive system, excretory system, kidneys, skin.

Ex 10

a it does so much work during the lifetime of a human
b 208 bones
c by a brain which is better than any computer imaginable
d kidneys
e with skin (containing 2–3 million sweat glands)
f our muscles

Ex 11

Nouns	Adjectives
skeleton	skeletal
muscle	muscular
blood	bloody
brain	brainy/brainless
skin	skinny
sweat	sweaty

bloody = covered in blood; also often used as a near-taboo word to express anger (e.g. "You bloody fool!")
brainy = intelligent; *brainless* = stupid
skinny = very thin
skeletal = very thin, emaciated

Ex 12
Open exercise

Ex 13

a head
b arm
c hand
d foot
e heart
f face
g stomach
h skin
i face
j neck
k head and shoulders
l heart

Ex 14, 15
Open exercises

UNIT 2
PHYSICAL APPEARANCE AND DESCRIPTION

Ex 1
Open exercise

Ex 2

Hair	Eyes	Nose	Mouth	Chin
dark thinning	dark			weak
		pointed		pointed
curly shiny		shiny		
	wide		wide	
	mean		mean	
receding				receding
	large bright protruding	large	large	
				strong
			generous	
				square
straight wiry		straight		
	appealing			

Ex 3
Open exercise

Ex 4

a fear, shock
b embarrassment
c fear, emotional excitement
d suspicion, disapproval
e wonder, emotional excitement, fear
f determination, disapproval
g determination

Ex 5
Open exercise

Ex 6
Open exercise

Ex 7

a He used to be muscular and slim; now he is a little overweight, quite plump
b He feels that she is not attractive in the conventional Cantonese sense, because her face contains too much expression, and in general she is quite big. On the other hand, he has noticed that she is attractive to Westerners

Ex 8

a lean
b sinewy
c plump
d thin
e chubby
f horsey

Ex 9, 10

Open exercises

Ex 11

Pleasant	Neutral	Unpleasant
slim	slight	skinny
slender	thin	emaciated
	underweight	
chubby	stout	fat
plump	obese	flabby
	overweight	

Note, however, that the connotation depends on context. A 'chubby baby' has pleasant connotations, but a 'chubby, middle-aged teacher' may be neutral. 'Obese' is a neutral medical term, but it can be used with negative connotations: e.g. 'He's rather overweight, isn't he?' 'Overweight? He's obese!'

Ex 12

Male only	Female only	Male and/or female
lean	voluptuous	tanned
handsome	nubile	muscular
beard	shapely	well-built
moustache	pretty	good-looking
	beautiful	attractive
	plain	ugly
		hideous
		glasses
		eyebrows

Ex 13

Open exercise

Ex 14

1 b   2 a   3 b   4 a   5 b   6 a

Ex 15

Open exercise

UNIT 3
CLOTHING

Ex 1

The words that can be combined with *dressed* are:
well-, casually, badly, over-, smartly, untidily
scruffy = untidily dressed/badly dressed
elegant = well-dressed, smartly dressed
dishevelled = untidily dressed
relaxed = casually dressed

Ex 2

Open exercise

Ex 3

	Transitive	Intransitive	Human subject	Inanimate subject
dress	✓	✓	✓	x
fit	✓	✓	x	✓
get dressed	x	✓	✓	x
put on	✓	x	✓	x
try on	✓	x	✓	x
suit	✓	x	x	✓
take off	✓	x	✓	x
undress	✓	✓	✓	x
wear	✓	x	✓	x

Ex 4, 5

Open exercises

Ex 6

(suggested answers)
The items being worn are:

trousers (AR, C)	knickers/panties (AS, D)
t-shirt (C)	pants (AR, C)
vest (AR?)	jeans (C)
blouse (D)	socks (AR, C, D?)
bra (AS, D)	bow tie (AR)
shorts (D)	sari (AS)
boxer shorts (AR? D?)	shoes (D, AR, AS, C)
tights (AS?)	stockings (AS?)

Ex 7

on the top half of the body only: T-shirt, vest, blouse, cardigan, bra, sweater, leather jacket, dinner jacket, waistcoat, anorak, sweatshirt
on the bottom half of the body only: trousers, shorts, boxer shorts, tights, jeans, skirt, pants, knickers/panties
on the top and the bottom halves of the body: dress, leotard, nightdress, raincoat, overcoat, fur coat, tracksuit, dressing gown, suit, pyjamas, sari
as underwear: vest, bra, boxer shorts, knickers/panties, pants
on the feet or legs: boots, tennis shoes, socks, shoes, stockings
in bed: nightdress, pyjamas
round the neck or on the head: tie, bow tie, shawl, scarf
when the weather is cold or wet: cardigan, sweater, raincoat, anorak

Ex 8
Open exercise

Ex 9
a in the same situation
b be in the opposite situation
c make an effort
d don't get over-excited
e be in charge
f talking rubbish
g look gentler than you are
h very smartly dressed, smartest clothes, special smart clothes
i get upset

Ex 10
You would expect to find an article like this in a magazine or a newspaper (in fact it's from the fashion column of a local English newspaper)

Ex 11
a tracksuit
b casual
d designers
e wool

c suit
f fabrics

Ex 12
a crisp, exhilarating and enjoyable
b a rich harvest to choose from
c the weather doesn't behave as it should
d until now
e it's a winning formula

Ex 13
(suggested answers – note that it is often difficult to find exact synonyms/antonyms)

	Synonym	Antonym
stylish	fashionable	sloppy
casual	informal/scruffy	smart/formal
lightweight	cool	thick/heavy
simple	staightforward	complex
beautifully		
styled	well cut	badly styled/cut
flattering	x really suits you	unflattering
alluring	attractive/sexy	unattractive/plain
naked	nude/bare	clothed

Ex 14
(suggested answers)
a stylish
b casual
c scruffy
d smart
e alluring
f naked

Ex 15, 16
Open exercises

UNIT 4
HEALTH AND EXERCISE

Ex 1, 2
Open exercises

Ex 3
a physically healthy and strong
b he looks extremely healthy
c not used to physical exercise, and so not strong
d in very good physical condition – and confident
e quite healthy
f in extremely good physical condition

g not used to physical exercise and so not strong/healthy

Ex 4
Open exercise

Ex 5
do: weight training; aerobics; yoga
play: golf; badminton
go: jogging; cycling; rowing

Ex 6
gym: weight training; aerobics
studio: yoga; aerobics
track: jogging; cycling
court: badminton
course: golf
outdoors: all of them

Ex 7
aerobic fitness: rowing, cross-country skiing, running/jogging, walking, golf, cycling or using an exercise cycle
muscle tone: weight training (pumping iron)

Ex 8
a 30 minute run: a run which lasts for half an hour
to work out: to do exercises like weight training etc
four-limb sports: sports in which you have to use both arms and both legs (like rowing)
lose weight: get rid of fat from the body
pumping iron: using weight training equipment
aerobic stamina: the ability to absorb oxygen well and carry out exercise for a long time
calorie: a unit for measuring energy available or used
energy: the power your body uses when it's working
warm-up: gentle exercises to prepare for physical exertion

a four-limb sports
b energy – in calories
c is 350 calories
d warm-up – you work out

e pumping iron – increase aerobic fitness

Ex 9
a press up
b sit up
c squat jumps
d skipping
e touching (your) toes

Ex 10
Open exercise

Ex 11
(suggested answers)
a She's using a rowing machine. This should keep her fit and tone up all her muscles
b She's touching her toes. This will strengthen her back and stomach muscles
c He's doing press-ups. This will develop his arm and shoulder muscles even more
d He's using an exercise cycle. This should help him to lose weight
e She's doing aerobics, which should keep her fit if she does it regularly
f They're jogging/going for a jog. This should increase their general fitness and stamina

Ex 12
a down on **b** on **c** on **d** up **e** on

Ex 13
Open exercise

Ex 14
a fascination with death is unhealthy
b the project looks in good shape
c he's not fit to hold office
d subjected to a daily diet of violence
e not got the stamina for the job
f despite.....she's got a healthy appetite

Ex 15
a fit
b unhealthy
c healthy
d stamina
e shape
f diet

Ex 16
Open exercise

UNIT 5
SICKNESS AND CURE

Ex 1

sprained	ankle, wrist, shoulder
broken	leg, ankle, arm, wrist, toe, finger
twisted	ankle, shoulder, finger
fractured	[as 'broken' + skull]
pulled	muscle
torn	ligament
black	eye
dislocated	shoulder, arm, finger
swollen	all except: skull, ligament, muscle
bruised	all except: ligament, muscle

Ex 2

Open exercise

Ex 3

a surgeon
b doctor
c nurse
d psychiatrist
e dentist
f optician

Ex 4

a the use of a special needle to give someone medicine – doctor or nurse
b a short letter which the doctor writes to say that you have been/are ill – doctor
c the taking of a small amount of blood to examine it in a laboratory – doctor or nurse
d checking to find out whether you can see and read properly, or to find out what kind of glasses you need – optician
e a piece of paper signed by the doctor that allows you to buy restricted medicines and drugs – doctor
f metal compound which the dentist uses to fill holes in your teeth – dentist
g the cutting of the body to put something right or remove a diseased part – surgeon
h treatment with electricity given to some patients with depression and other psychiatric illnesses – psychiatrist

Ex 5

Open exercise

Ex 6

a i) can mean 'I've vomited'
   ii) 'I've not been well'
b i) 'I've got a pain in my hand'
   ii) 'My hand has been damaged – I can't use it properly'
c i) 'six people were hurt in such a way that their skin was broken and they bled'
   ii) 'six people were hurt in some other way, probably without the skin being broken (e.g. fractures, bruises, concussion etc.)'
d i) 'The skin on my hand is irritated, because of a mosquito, for example'
   ii) 'I have a pain in my hand'

Ex 7

a sick
b itching
c wounded
d ill
e hurting

Ex 8

The marriage between Charles and Matilda had been a mistake. He didn't love her, and perhaps there was some secret in his past...

Ex 9

The words are all used metaphorically: the two people aren't physically 'ill', 'sick' etc. but their emotions make them feel that way

Ex 10

Open exercise

Ex 11

A: Good morning.
B: Hello, Doctor.
A: Now then, how can I help you?
B: Well, doctor, I'm not feeling very well. I've got these awful pains in my stomach and I haven't been sleeping at all well.
A: Do you have any other symptoms? A temperature, for example?
B: Well, yes. I have had a bit of a temperature, actually.
A: Mmm. It looks to me as if you've got some kind of a stomach infection.
B: Oh, have I, Doctor?
A: Yes. Now I'm going to give you these pills. I

want you to take two pills three times a day.
B: Thank you, Doctor. Thank you.

Ex 12

a physical and other signs of an illness
b feeling ill
c beginning to feel ill
d an infection in the throat which causes a lot of
pain
e my chest is hurting
f a fever (above 37 degrees)
g a problem caused by a virus or bacteria
h tablets sold at the chemist's
i a lot of relaxation (e.g. in bed)

Ex 13

Open exercise

Ex 14

a hurting   e operation
b injection   f took out
c nurse   g condition
d bear   h pull through

Ex 15

Open exercise

Unit 6
AGES AND AGEING

Ex 1

a Open exercise
b e.g. wrinkled, good-natured, kind, fussy, unsteady

Ex 2

Open exercise

Ex 3

a grow up
b childish
c grown-up
d you're old enough to know better

Ex 4, 5

Open exercises

Ex 6

See artwork for suggested answer on page
178.

Ex 7

State (noun)	State (adj)	Person (noun)
adolescence	adolescent	adolescent
retirement	retired	retired person
maturity	mature	mature person
infancy	infant	infant
womanhood	womanly	woman
manhood	manly	man
youth	youthful	youth
childhood	child-like	child

Ex 8

(suggested answers)
a Yes, she's absolutely *ancient*.
b Yes, he's just a *baby/an infant*.
c Yes, he's rather *childish*.
d No, I'm not. I'm quite *grown up*.
e Oh, really. I think he's rather *mature* for his age.
f I don't agree. I've always thought of myself as
youthful.

Ex 9

(suggested answers)
wisdom – old age; *exuberance* – childhood;
creativity – youth, maturity; *attractiveness* – youth.
the opposites of these qualities are:
foolishness
sluggishness
lack of creativity
ugliness

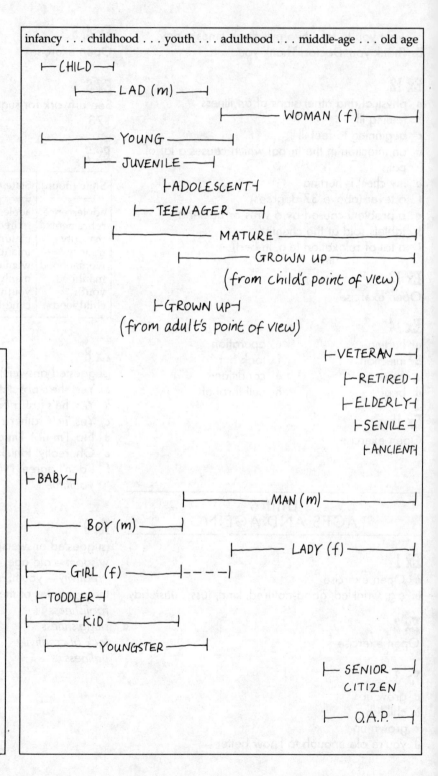

infancy . . . childhood . . . youth . . . adulthood . . . middle-age . . . old age

├─ CHILD ─┤
├──── LAD (m) ────┤
├──────── WOMAN (f) ───────┤
├───────── YOUNG ─────────┤
├──── JUVENILE ────┤
├ADOLESCENT┤
├── TEENAGER ──┤
├──────────── MATURE ────────────┤
├──────── GROWN UP ────────┤
(from child's point of view)
├GROWN UP┤
(from adult's point of view)
├VETERAN─┤
├RETIRED┤
├ELDERLY┤
├SENILE┤
├ANCIENT┤
├BABY┤
├───── MAN (m) ─────┤
├──── BOY (m) ────┤
├───── LADY (f) ─────┤
├──── GIRL (f) ────┤- - - -┤
├TODDLER┤
├──── KID ────┤
├───── YOUNGSTER ─────┤
├─ SENIOR ─┤
CITIZEN
├─ O.A.P. ─┤

Notice that many of these words can be used to describe people's behaviour or attitudes and, in this case, are not linked to a particular physical age.

For example, although *young* and *youngster* are often used to describe children and teenagers, they can also be used of older people.
e.g. Middle-aged man: "I must be getting really old, all the policemen look like teenagers!"
Octogenarian: "Nonsense! You're only a youngster!"

Veteran can be used to describe anyone with long experience in something. e.g. a Vietnam war veteran, a veteran public speaker.

Mature can be used of anyone with a grown-up and sensible attitude, e.g. 'He's very mature for a ten-year-old.'

Girl is often used to refer to older women, but many find this offensive.

Ex 10

(suggested answers)
All of these expressions can be used in an ironical
way. The degree of irony or seriousness will
depend on the situation.

a = too old for the activity I have in mind.
b = is becoming (or behaves as if he/she is)
    middle-aged. [could be a compliment if the
    person is over 40]
c = not young or youthful
d = at a very creative and powerful stage in her
    life or career
e = The 'sell-by date' appears on food packaging
    etc. This could mean the person is no longer in
    his/her prime
f = seems old or too old for a given activity
g = seems very old or unwell
h = seems very young (for a given activity)
i = appears less mature than he is
j = seems old or too old for a given activity

All the expressions are informal or colloquial British
English.

Ex 11

a juvenile   d veteran
b seasoned   e grow up
c mature   f youthful

Ex 12

a neutral   f neutral
b unpleasant   g pleasant
c unpleasant   h neutral
d pleasant   i unpleasant
e neutral

Ex 13

Open exercise

Ex 14

Suggested answer:
The poems both seem to be about old people. In
the first poem the poet is shocked by the way
Stania has aged, not having seen him for a long
time, but in the second the couple are growing old
together.

Ex 15, 16, 17

Open exercises

UNIT 7
BIRTH AND DEATH

Ex 1

Houghton – announces a birth
Robertson – announces a death

The people and places are:
a the hospital
b the father
c the mother's family name before she got married
d the deceased
e the widow
f the deceased's children

Ex 2, 3

Open exercises

Ex 4

You are conceived
You are born
You get pregnant
You give birth
You die
Not much of a story,
Is it?

Ex 5

1 became   5 labour
2 expecting   6 caesarian
3 contractions   7 born
4 birth   8 given

Ex 6

birth control   birthplace
birthmark   birthright
birthrate

Ex 7

a five   d four
b three   e two
c six
Identical twins are two children born to a woman
at the same time who look very alike.

Ex 8

Open exercise

Ex 9

a kick the bucket, pass on
b the deceased, dear departed
c at peace

Ex 10

a from
b of
c after
d in
e from/as a result of
f of
g in
h of

Ex 11

Verb	Noun	Adjective	Past Participle
die	death	dying	died
live	life	living	lived
be born	birth	xxxxx	born

Ex 12

a death; died
b dying
c death
d dying
e dead
f died
g death (or dying)

Fixed phrase: b, d
Metaphor: f

Ex 13

a fatal
b fatal
c deadly/lethal
d lethal
e deadly
f fatal

Ex 14

'Divers today...': drown
'Something she ate...': choke
'After the first...': to have a stroke
'He suddenly stood up...': to have a heart attack
'That's the problem...': to choke, suffocate
'We think the accident...': to be run over

Ex 15

Open exercise

Ex 16

(suggested answers)
Hamlet — poisoned
Macbeth — killed in a sword-fight
Pere Goriot — died of a stroke
Werther — shot himself

Ex 17

1 pregnant
2 conceived
3 birth
4 death
5 drowned
6 choked
7 heart attack
8 dying

Ex 18

Open exercise

Ex 19, 20

Open exercises

Ex 21

(possible explanations)

WIDOW SUES HOTEL COOK: The wife of somebody who has died (presumably of food poisoning) wants compensation from the cook who prepared his final meal.

MIRACLE OF FIRST BABY FOR PANDA HING-HING: A panda in a famous zoo has surprised the world by giving birth unexpectedly to a healthy baby.

SEXTUPLETS MUM ECSTATIC SAYS PROUD FATHER: A woman who has recently given birth to six healthy babies is extremely pleased, according to her husband.

DISTRAUGHT ROMEO IN SUICIDE BID: A man whose girlfriend recently left him for someone else is recovering in hospital after attempting to kill himself.

FATAL DISEASE THREATENS SEAL POPULATION: Experts are baffled by the cause of a mystery illness which is killing thousands of seals.

UNIT 8
WAKING AND SLEEPING

Ex 1

to wake up: to stop sleeping

to go to sleep: to start sleeping

nap: a short sleep (usually in the daytime, probably not in bed)

a siesta: a short sleep after lunch

a light sleeper: someone who wakes easily

a heavy sleeper: someone who wakes with difficulty

to snore: to make a snorting noise while sleeping

to sleepwalk: to get out of bed and walk around without waking

to talk in your sleep: to speak or shout while sleeping

to grind your teeth: to rub the upper teeth against the lower teeth, making a noise.

to dream: to have uncontrolled fantasies while sleeping

to have a nightmare: to have a bad or frightening dream

to fall into a deep sleep: to go to sleep and sleep soundly

to toss and turn: to find it difficult to sleep, and so move around in the bed

to sleep like a log: to sleep very soundly

to get to sleep: to begin sleeping

to get back to sleep: to begin sleeping again after having woken up

to oversleep: to sleep longer than intended

Ex 2, 3, 4

Open exercises

Ex 5

(suggested answers)

As a 'duke' is mentioned and as nobody seems to be doing very much, they could be aristocrats or wealthy people.

'A fire in the grate' is mentioned, and there is a rider near the house, so the period probably isn't contemporary. But it doesn't seem to be long ago either.

Something dramatic is obviously going to happen.

Ex 6

Awake: Sarah, Lloyd, the Duke, Vivian

Asleep: Old George, Mrs Middle

Ex 7

conscious: Sarah, Lloyd, the Duke, Vivian

reverie: Sarah, Lloyd

catnap: Old George, Mrs Middle

Ex 8

wide: awake

fast: asleep

fully: awake, alert, conscious

sound: asleep

half: asleep, awake, conscious

semi-: alert, conscious

Ex 9

Open exercise

Ex 10

Vocabulary will probably be required as follows:

a tossing and turning, couldn't get to sleep

b overslept, couldn't wake up

c wide awake, fully alert

d sound asleep, slept like a log

e woke up, dream, nightmare

Ex 11

sleeping, sleepy, sleepless; waking; dreaming, dream-like, dreamless; nightmarish, dozy, trance-like

Ex 12

a	sleeping	d dream-like
b	waking	e trance-like
c	nightmarish	f dreamless

Ex 13

a	dreams	f dream
b	wake up	g sleep
c	sleeping	h sleep
d	sleep	i dream
e	nightmare	j sleep

Ex 14

a	h	f	a
b	e	g	j
c	g	h	i
d	d	i	b
e	c	j	f

Ex 15

Expressions will probably be required as follows:
a put to sleep/sleep it off
b sleep on it
c waking up from a nightmare
d sleeping partner/waking nightmare

Ex 16

Open exercise

UNIT 9
WALKING AND RUNNING

Ex 1

hangover: a headache and a feeling of being ill the day after drinking too much

jogger: a person who runs regularly to keep fit.

sidewalk: (American English) the path beside a road where pedestrians can walk – 'pavement' in British English

tailcoat: a jacket with long 'tails' at the back which is worn on certain formal occasions

Bourbon: a type of whisky made in the U.S.

archery: a sport which involves shooting arrows at a target

fog: a thick mist, like a cloud

klaxons: horn or hooter of a car etc., used for warning others to get out of the way

limped: walked unevenly because of an injury or disability in one leg or foot

fell: came down from a standing position (e.g. because of an accident)

Ex 2

Open exercise

Ex 3

The correct answer was (b).

Ex 4

(suggested answer)
He seems to be someone who lives in a disorganized and maybe dissolute way. He seems to live alone and to be rather unhealthy. He had probably slept in his clothes. They are probably untidy, creased and quite old and dirty.

Ex 5

Open exercise

Ex 6, 7

	Walk	Run
slowly and with difficulty	staggered limped stumbled plod totter hobble lurch	
trying not to make a noise	tiptoe creep pad	
looking ridiculous and/or clumsy	shuffling waddle	
in a showing-off kind of way	strut swagger	
showing anger or strong decision	strode stomp march pace	
slowly and with pleasure	sauntered stroll wander sidle	
as fast as possible		sprinted dashed
at a reasonable speed for training		jog

Ex 8

(suggested answers)
a He sidled up to her/sauntered over to her
b She dashed into the station/along the platform

c He staggered/lurched/tottered/limped up the
   street towards his house
d He wandered lonely as a cloud of...
e She crept/tiptoed downstairs and...
f He strode/marched into his office...
g They dashed/sprinted across the playground
h He paced up and down outside the room
i She lurched/tottered across the room

Ex 9

purposefully: stride, march
aimlessly: saunter, stroll, wander, shuffle
nervously: tiptoe, creep
painfully: stagger, limp, hobble, shuffle, waddle
awkwardly: stumble, hobble, shuffle, waddle
angrily: stride, stomp, march
confidently: strut, swagger, stride, march, sidle
unsteadily: stagger, totter, lurch, shuffle, waddle
cautiously: tiptoe, creep, shuffle

Ex 10
Open exercise

Ex 11

a I'm running away from my parents
b I ran into my cousin in the High Street
c We've run out of sugar
d They ran the sheriff out of town
e I'll run you up a skirt
f Oh no! Did we run over that cat?

Ex 12

a correct: 'run over' is a separable phrasal verb.
b correct: you can 'run up' something in writing as
   well as a piece of clothing etc.
c incorrect: phrasal-prepositional verbs are not
   separable, so it should read 'I am running
   away from my wife'.
d incorrect: 'run into' is a prepositional verb so it
   isn't separable. It should read 'I ran into my
   friend the other day'.

Ex 13
Open exercise

Ex 14

a *made my blood run cold:* made me very
   frightened/terrified
b *will run and run:* will be very successful and will
   keep going a long time
c *run your eye over:* look at something quickly
d *run rings round:* be much more successful
   than/successfully manipulate
e *let someone walk all over you:* allow someone
   to treat you badly
f *run riot:* behave in a very uncontrolled way
g *walk right into something:* get into trouble
   without expecting it

Ex 15
Open exercise

Ex 16

a	2	e	8
b	1	f	1
c	6	g	3
d	4, 5	h	7

Ex 17, 18
Open exercises

Ex 19
(possible answer)
He crept nervously into the room. I could see that
he was....

UNIT 10
BODY LANGUAGE AND
MOVEMENT

Ex 1

a	bowing	d	curtseying
b	bowing	e	kneeling
c	kneeling	f	kneeling

Ex 2
Open exercise

Ex 3

a hands, arms, legs
b head, shoulders
c fist, hand, teeth

d finger
e finger, hand, arm, leg, eyebrows, hips, shoulders, ears
f finger
g arms, legs
h shoulders
i shoulders
j head
k all except teeth and ears
l arms, legs
m head, fist, finger, hands, arms, legs

Ex 4

a clenched
b shook
c nodded
d shrugged
e raised
f raised
g folded/crossed

Ex 5

a raising your eyebrows
b clenching your fist
c waving your arms, raising your hand
d crossing/folding your arms
e nodding your head
f wiggling your hips
g shrugging your shoulders

Ex 6

Open exercise

Ex 7

(suggested answers)
a The man is wagging his finger at the girl. He's angry with her
b The elderly man is shrugging his shoulders as if to say "it's not my fault"
c The woman is stroking her chin. She seems to be trying to make a decision
d The model is posing seductively, presumably for a photograph
e The woman is shaking her fist at the other driver. She must be angry with him
f The girl is raising her hand. She wants to ask the teacher something
g The man is gesturing to the policeman. He must be trying to explain something
h The woman is pointing to the door. She wants the man to leave

Ex 8

Open exercise

Ex 9

1 Peregrine
2 Caroline
3 Jim
4 Pamela
5 Mary
6 The Colonel
7 Sara
8 Jessica
9 Martin

Ex 10

Open exercise

Ex 11

a pushed
b carried
c reached
d stretching
e pulled
f dragged

Ex 12

(possible answers)
a I would drag it/push it on a trolley
b drag some furniture to the middle of the room, stand on it, stretch my arms up . . .
c (almost anything)

Ex 13

a drag
b bent
c reach
d push
e pulled
f reach
g bow

Ex 14

a bow to your judgement
b bent over backwards
c reach an agreement
d drag her name through the mud
e don't push me
f don't reach for the stars
g pulled in two different directions

Ex 15

(possible answers)
C: Look, can we talk about this and . . .
F: I'm sorry, I can't see the good name of the company being dragged through the mud.
C: It won't be, I promise. You've got to see it from my side. I'm sure we can reach an agreement.

F: Look, I've bent over backwards to do my best for you, and now I find out that you've been messing around with terrorists . . .

C: They're not terrorists, they're freedom fighters . . .

F: You're just playing with words. I can't bow to your authority on this, although you are my brother-in-law and I'm being pulled in two directions . . .

C: Come on, give me a break. I've done a lot for you. If you keep quiet no-one will know, and it's all in a good cause . . .

F: Don't push me . . . I'm going home to think this through.

UNIT 11
THE MIND AND THINKING

Ex 1
Open exercise

Ex 2

think about something carefully and for a longtime, without necessarily coming to a conclusion. ponder (T), reflect (on), consider (T), meditate (on), deliberate (for/ . . .)
come to a tentative conclusion about something, based on limited evidence and maybe personal opinion. guess (T), suppose (that), assume (that), reckon (that/ . . .)
come to a conclusion about something after examining all the evidence and facts. conclude (from), infer (from), judge (T), weigh up (T)
find out by scientific examination or calculation. analyse (T), assess (T), work out (T)

Ex 3

guess N	judge N
suppose F	reflect F
assess F	infer F
ponder F	consider N
assume N	weigh up I
analyse N	deliberate F
conclude N	reckon I
work out I	meditate N

Ex 4
a nouns

-tion/-sion	-ence	-ing	-ment
reflection deliberation meditation assumption conclusion supposition consideration	inference	reckoning	assessment judgement

b *meditative:* quietly, thoughtful, *conclusive:* definite; there can be no doubt.

Ex 5
(suggested answers)
a Did you conclude that the experiment had failed?
b Who analysed the results?
c. Joan pondered deeply the implications of the changes
d We considered the matter carefully
e It took him a long time to work it out
f He seemed to be meditating
g What can we infer from this discussion?
h I suppose Diana has gone to see Andy
i Upon reflection Sally accepted the job

Ex 6
Open exercise

Ex 7
a brain, logic, intelligence
b thought, mind
c ideas, impression, notion, mentality
d memory

Ex 8
(suggested answers)
a what ideas/possibilities have you thought of?
b decide
c I've almost decided
d I'm worrying about something
e please would you, would you be unhappy if you . . .
f be careful/look out!
g concentrate/if you are determined to do it

Ex 9
Open exercise

Ex 10
(suggested answers)

Out of sight out of mind means when someone/ something isn't actually there in front of you you don't think about them/it.

Mind over matter means that you force yourself (not) to do something by willpower even though your body (doesn't) want(s) to do it.

Great minds think alike is an expression that we use when we want to complement someone else and ourselves because we share the same opinion.

Ex 11

	Person	Idea
logical	✓	✓
pensive	✓	
thoughtful	✓	
thoughtless	✓	
aware	✓	
reasonable	✓	✓
unreasonable	✓	✓
mental	✓	
psychological	✓	
brainy	✓	✓
brainless	✓	
conceptual	✓	
conscious		✓
unconscious	✓	✓
intelligent	✓	✓
intellectual	✓	✓
considerate	✓	
clever	✓	✓

the way a person treats other people: thoughtful, thoughtless, considerate
intelligent: brainy, clever (intellectual?)

Ex 12
a pensive, thoughtful
b thoughtful, considerate
c mental
d conscious/aware
e brainy, intelligent, clever
f thoughtless (unreasonable?)
g unreasonable
h unconscious
i logical, (intelligent)

Ex 13
Dialogue 1:
I have lovely memories of our college days.
— Yes, me too. Whenever we meet it all comes back to me.
I'll never forget the day you got drunk and fell down the stairs, for example.
— Really? Down the stairs? I have no recollection of the incident.
You were in love with someone called Angela, as I recall. That's what caused it.
— I need something to jog my memory. What was Angela like?
Don't you remember? She had dark brown hair and brown eyes. A real beauty if my memory serves me well.
— My mind's a blank, but it's possible that you're right.
What do you mean: it's possible that I'm right?
Here's a photo of you at the bottom of the stairs as a permanent reminder.

Dialogue 2:
Hallo. Didn't you say you would meet us at 6.30? Or is my memory playing tricks?
— Did I? I've got a mind like a sieve, I'm afraid. I thought I said 7 o'clock.
And where's Joe? I hope he hasn't forgotten all about the meeting. He's so absent-minded these days.
— It's getting really late now. Where can he be? He's so forgetful.
By the way, I was racking my brains trying to think of Joe's surname. What is it?
— Erm ... it's on the tip of my tongue: Donaldson or Davidson I think.
Perhaps we'd better phone to remind him. Who can remember his phone number?
— It looks as if no-one has remembered to bring it. What a memorable meeting we're having.

Remembers/remembered	Doesn't/didn't remember
I'll never forget the day as I recall I can remember it as if it was yesterday if my memory serves me well a permanent reminder memorable it all comes back to me	racking my brains absent-minded a mind like a sieve forgetful my mind's a blank on the tip of my tongue jog my memory I have no recollection of . . .

Ex 14
Open exercise

UNIT 12
PERCEPTION AND THE SENSES

Ex 1
Open exercise

Ex 2
(suggested answers)
'Gestalt' means the belief that what we see doesn't depend on what things actually are but on the processes in the brain which are present at birth.

Ex 3

Nouns	Adjectives	Verbs
psychologist	psychological	
theory	theoretical	theorize
perception	perceptive	perceive
outline	outlined	outline
demonstration	demonstrative	demonstrate
experience	experiential	experience
sense	sensory	sense
image		imagine
process		process

Ex 4
a demonstrate
b process
c theory
d sense
e image

Ex 5
a saw – because it happened suddenly without any intention on our part
b looking at, watching – because obviously B is doing the watching on purpose
c watch – the speaker may see televisions as he or she passes a shop, but doesn't actually choose to watch what's on
d look at, see – the first speaker is asking D to choose to look, but D can't make the choice because he or she doesn't know where to look, hence 'see'

e hear, listen, see – the first action is involuntary, the second needs choice, the third 'see' = discover
f saw, looked at – saw is involuntary, looked at here means a 'voluntary' stare

look at, watch, listen to

Ex 6
a 4 – she stared at him in absolute horror (L)
b 6 – She glanced at him quickly to see if he had heard (S)
c 8 – She gazed at him in deep admiration (N)
d 9 – she observed the people on the beach below carefully (L)
e 3 – She noticed a small crack she hadn't seen before (S)
f 7 – she spotted a face she recognised in the crowd (S)
g 10 – She scanned the pages of the newspaper in case there was a report on the meeting (N)
h 2 – She peered at the building through the fog (N)
i 5 – she peeped through a crack in the door to see inside (S)
j 1 – She glimpsed the red Mercedes as it flashed by (S)

Ex 7
(example story)
Mark needed to find a new flat so he scanned the pages of the newspaper (for advertisements about flats to rent). He found one that looked suitable so he rang the number in the paper and made an appointment to see the place. As he was going up the stairs a young woman rushed past him. She stared at him in shock and Mark caught a glimpse of blood on her hand. He ran up to the flat and knocked on the door but there was no answer. He peeped through the keyhole but he couldn't see anything unusual although he did smell smoke. He broke down the door and peered across the room, his eyes full of tears caused by the smoke. Mark put out the fire and glanced round the room; there was absolute chaos. He went into the bedroom and found himself gazing in horror at the body on the floor; it – he – was a man with a kitchen knife in his back in a pool of blood. Mark spotted the telephone under the bed and called the police

before closing the eyes of the victim which had been staring at him penetratingly.

Strangely enough Mark decided not to take the flat.

Ex 8
(possible answers)
Taste – sweet (*sugar, candy*), sour (*lime, unripe fruit*), salty (*smoked fish*), hot (*chillies, curry*), like vinegar (*cheap wine*)
Feel – soft (*wool, down*), rough (*sandpaper, new jeans*), smooth (*glass, polished stone*), sticky (*honey, glue*), cold (*marble, ice*), like silk (*sheer stockings, expensive scarf*)
Smell – rotten (*bad egg, rubbish*), sweet (*toffee, cake being baked*), sweaty (*unwashed clothes, sports people after a tough game*), acrid (*smoke, acid*), like flowers (*perfume*)
Look – dangerous (*bull, gun*), ugly (*a decrepit old crone, a horrible expression*), frightening (*ghost, monster*), exciting (*a race, a new discovery*), relaxing (*an armchair, a comfortable bed*), like cheese (*the moon*)

Ex 9
(suggested order)
5 perfume, 4 fragrance, 3 aroma, 2 stench, 1 stink

Ex 10
Open exercise

Ex 11

You see them	You hear them
shine (2)	bang (2)
glow (1)	roar (3)
flash (3)	knock (1)
dazzle	pop (1)
glint (1)	crash (2)
glimmer (1)	bump (1)
glitter (2)	rustle (1)
	rumble (2)

Ex 12
a rumble, crash
b pop
c bang, dazzle, flash
d flash, glint, glimmer
e rustle
f flash
g dazzle
h bump
i roar
j crash
k glimmer

Ex 13
A: What do you think of my new car then?
B: I must say it's absolutely beautiful, *a sight for sore eyes*. It's a 1956 Jaguar, isn't it?
A: Yes. I *keep my eyes on* advertisements in the papers just in case there's a car I really want. And this one suddenly popped up. It was a bargain.
B: It certainly *sounds as if* you've found what you were looking for. How much was it if you don't mind my asking?
A: Only £8,000. *The way I look at it*, that was a reasonable price to pay.
B: £8,000 for an old car! You must have money to burn.
A: Well, you've got to *take a long-term view*: you've got to think of the future. It's better to buy a car which is going to increase in value than one which is going to lose value, in *my view*.
B: Is it really worth that much?
A: Yes. In fact the owner wanted £9,000 for it to start with, because he said it had only done 60,000 miles. But I *smelled a rat*, and in the end he admitted that 160,000 was nearer the truth. So he dropped the price.
B: And what's it like to drive?
A: Lovely. It's got a nice solid *feel to it*.
B: I must say I envy you. But spending that amount of money would certainly *leave a nasty taste* in my mouth.

Ex 14
Open exercise

UNIT 13
FEELINGS AND MOODS

Ex 1
The missing word is 'worry' (this can be deduced from the second half of the poem).

Ex 2, 3

Happy	Unhappy	Worried
glad *v*	anguished	anxious
thrilled *v*	depressed *v*	dismayed *v*
ecstatic	miserable	concerned *v*
pleased *v*	bored *v*	
delighted *v*	heartbroken *v*	
	upset *v*	

Angry	Afraid	Shocked
cross	nervous	astounded *v*
irritated *v*	apprehensive	appalled *v*
furious	frightened *v*	horrified *v*
livid	scared *v*	astonished *v*
	terrified *v*	

Ex 4
To describe his/her own feelings, the first speaker uses 'boring', which describes something (or somebody) that makes others feel bored.

'Bored' is the only adjective in this pair which can describe a person's feelings.

a appalled
b upsetting
c inhibited
d intimidating

Ex 5
a I find the news you have just given me astonishing
b She felt more and more irritated with every word he uttered
c The poor child found it so frightening when I burst the balloon that he/she leapt nearly three feet into the air
d I can't help feeling some anxiety about the future
e The puppet show delighted the children
f I worry about you all the time
g His rude behaviour appalls me
h Your arrival gladdens my heart

Ex 6
Open exercise

Ex 7
(possible answer)

Topics	Predictions
relationships	start, and, improve etc
work/study	harder, easier, successful
money	more, nice surprise, difficult
home-life	better, more problematic etc

Ex 8
a to d open exercises – depend on students' own answers to Ex 7
e Virgo

Ex 9
Open exercise

Ex 10
(possible answers)
a when I meet someone I don't like/who makes me angry
b when facing a problem or situation I have no experience of
c when I had done something dishonest or nasty, or had caused problems for others
d when someone is trying to persuade me to do something I definitely don't want to do
e when I am relaxed and happy – and pleased with myself
f when waiting for someone or something, especially if he/she/it is late
g when someone criticizes my personality or something I have done
h before an exam or some other tricky or new experience
i when something that I was looking forward to doesn't happen
j when talking to someone who is very good at the subject I'm talking about
k when dealing with something I know a lot about and can do well

190 *Answer key*

Ex 11

a unfriendliness
b inadequacy
c guilt
d stubbornness
e serenity
f impatience
g sensitivity
h nervousness
i disappointment
j intimidation
k strength

Ex 12

a unfriendly
b sensitive
c serenity
d inadequacy
e intimidated
f guilty
g stubborn
h disappointed

Ex 13
Open exercise

Ex 14

	Mood	Temper
to be in a good	✓	✓
to be in a bad	✓	✓
to be in an excellent	✓	
to be in a foul	✓	✓
to keep your		✓
to lose your		✓

Ex 15
(suggested answers)
He/she — went red in the face
— frowned
— clenched his/her teeth (and/or fists)
His/her eyes narrowed

Ex 16

Happy	Surprised	Not happy
Shiona	Tom	Marina
Chris	Will	Roger
Will	Sarah	

Ex 17
(suggested answers)
made me really mad: e, f
got me down: a, b, f
gives/gave me a buzz: a, c, g
took me completely by surprise: a, b, c, d, e, f, g
I was/am bowled over: a, c, f, g
I was/am caught off balance: c, d, e, f, g
I was/am over the moon: a, c, g

Ex 18
Open exercise

UNIT 14
LIKES AND DISLIKES

Ex 1
It seems to be about being in love (b)

Ex 2, 3
Open exercises

Ex 4, 5

Words connected with liking	Words connected with disliking
like	dislike
get a kick out of	hate
enjoy	detest
love	don't care for
be fond of	loathe
charming	not that keen on
be devoted to	can't stand
loveable	detestable
adorable	revolting
enchanting	hateful
captivating	odious
tempting	disgusting
enticing	repulsive
to fancy	
desirable	

Ex 6
Open exercise

Ex 7

Adjective	Noun	Verb
revolting	revulsion	to revolt
charming	charm	to charm
devoted	devotion	to devote
loveable	love	to love
adorable	adoration	to adore
enchanting	enchantment	to enchant
captivating	captivation	to captivate
tempting	temptation	to tempt
enticing	enticement	to entice
fanciable	fancy	to fancy
hateful	hate	to hate
disgusting	disgust	to disgust
desirable	desire	to desire
repulsive	repulsion	to repulse

Ex 8

a harmful
b disgusting
c captivated
d repulse
e temptation
f enticing
g loveable/detestable
h addicted

Ex 9

(suggested answers) vocabulary will probably be required as follows (adjectives only given – you can use nouns and verbs too)

a repulsive, disgusting, hateful
b charming, loveable
c revolting, disgusting, repulsive
d tempting, hateful, disgusting
e charming, enchanting, captivating

Ex 10

Verb	–ing verb	to+infinitive
like	✓	✓
love	✓	✓
hate	✓	✓
dislike	✓	x
detest	✓	x
enjoy	✓	x
loathe	✓	✓
adore	✓	x
be fond of	✓	x
can't stand	✓	x
(not) keen on	✓	x
don't care for	✓	x
be (really) into	✓	x

Ex 11

a ii **b** i **c** iii

Ex 12

a right
b wrong – 'absolutely' doesn't go with 'keen' – 'very' does
c right but 'really' would sound better, perhaps
d wrong – 'quite' is positive but 'loathe' is negative 'rather loathe' is possible (but unlikely)
e right
f wrong – 'fairly' can only be used with adjectives/adverbs
g right

Ex 13

a fairly, quite
b absolutely, really, simply
c rather (the difference often depends on intonation)

'fairly' cannot be used before a verb, only with an adjective or adverb

Ex 14

Open exercise

Ex 15

Likes Ralph's music	is neutral	doesn't like it
Paul	Kate	Anne
Liz	Brian	Irma
Keith	Jenny	
Tim		
John		

Ex 16, 17

Open exercises

UNIT 15
CHARACTER AND PERSONALITY 1

Ex 1, 2

Open exercises

Ex 3

a The author would have to admit that 70% of American tourists are 'regrettable' (they are uncultured, lack historical sense, are concerned only with business, have no sensitivity and ought to stay at home). In general they are worse than the English.

b Others tend to describe all Americans as all of (a) above but also they are loud, have no manners, no education, no sense of proportion. They are offensively vulgar in dress, speech, eating habits, and general comportment.

Ex 4

a the author is American and he makes this clear with statements like '. . . I could not logically protest', 'I would have to admit that . . . the American is worse'.

b Open exercise

c He dislikes it when they say that 100% of a certain nationality behave in a certain way because it is 'false to the facts'.

d He seems to suggest that you can not say that all people of the same nationality have the same 'national character'.

Ex 5

a cultivated – 'uncultured'
sensitive – 'had no sensitivity'
good-mannered – 'had no manners'
quiet – 'loud'
refined – 'offensively vulgar'
generous – 'mean'
modest – 'arrogant'
admirable – 'regrettable'

b uncultured – Americans
had no manners – Americans
loud – Americans
offensively vulgar – Americans
mean – Frenchmen
arrogant – Swedes
regrettable – Americans

c possible opposites for some of the words include: reserved – flamboyant, lively – lazy, polite – aggressive, boring – fun, hard-working – lazy, inflexible – eccentric, inscrutable – frank, cheerful – reserved, hypocritical – genuine.

Ex 6

a Open exercise

b 1 American   2 Chinese   3 British
4 Japanese   5 French   6 Brazilian
7 Swiss   8 Russian

Ex 7

Positive	Negative	Positive or negative
patience	mischief	ferocity
grace	evil	play
serenity	stupidity	pride
gentleness	vanity	cunning
loyalty	greed	independence
bravery	deceit	cleverness
	obstinacy	
	cowardice	

Ex 8

(suggested answers)

a obstinate
b vain
c modest
d graceful
e mischevious
f patient
g cunning (deceitful)
h loyal

Ex 9

a Open exercise

b Open exercise (but the following tend to be only associated with humans: serenity, pride, vanity, deceit, obstinacy, modesty).

Ex 10

boastful: snobbish, arrogant, overbearing, conceited
tolerant: impartial, objective, fair, long suffering
loving: affectionate, devoted
violent: barbarous, sadistic
brave: heroic, fearless, courageous
hard-working: diligent, industrious, conscientious

Ex 11

a Diana
b Mr Brown
c Sally
d David
e Miriam
f Luke
g Mike
h Tom

Ex 12
Open exercise

UNIT 16
CHARACTER AND PERSONALITY 2

Ex 1
Open exercise

Ex 2
Open exercise

Ex 3
Positive: (adjectives) energetic, sociable, (nouns) willpower, hard worker
Negative: (adjectives) impatient, selfish, indecisive, boring, moody, disorganized, absent-minded, stupid
Neutral: active, ambitious, fun-loving, calm, cool, easy-going, shy, forgetful, nervous, articulate, restless, (nouns) anxiety, self-confidence

Ex 4
energy, sociability, impatience, selfishness, indecision, boredom, mood, disorganization, absent-mindedness, stupidity, action, ambition, calm, shyness, forgetfulness, nervousness, articulateness, restlessness

Ex 5
lethargic – energetic, confident – nervous, clever – stupid, magnanimous – selfish, excitable – calm, lazy – active/energetic

Ex 6
Open exercise

Ex 7
a (suggested answer) Mary Wollstonecraft seems to have been someone who was fiercely independent and extremely tough and passionate. But she was also almost a manic depressive, with violent swings of mood.
b Open exercise

Ex 8
((√) = author approves, (×) = weaknesses) ebullient (√), enthusiasm (√), frequently opinionated (×), passionate (√), reliance on her own judgement (√), sense of futility and loneliness (×), sense of her own independence (√), suicidal depression (×)

Ex 9

Adjectives	Nouns
moody	mood
emotional	emotion
desperate	despair
likeable	xxxxx
prejudiced	prejudice
affectionate	affection
passionate	passion
charming	charm
optimistic	optimism
pessimistic	pessimism
carefree	xxxxx
warm-hearted	warm heart
vivacious	vivacity
lively	liveliness
anxious	anxiety
enthusiastic	enthusiasm
independent	independence
unstable	instability
domineering	xxxxx
lonely	loneliness

Ex 10
a sociable/charming
b charm
c optimism
d anxious
e enthusiastic/carefree/vivacious
f prejudices
g enthusiasm
h lonely
i independent

Ex 11
The correct order for B's lines in the dialogue is:
1 – 5 – 4 – 3 – 2

Ex 12, 13
Open exercises

Contents

Acknowledgements

We would like to thank Sue Maingay for her help and encouragement during the writing of these materials and Jane Walsh for her constructive comments. Thanks also to Alison Steadman for all her work.

As the work has gradually evolved we have been lucky in the excellent reports that we have received from Janet Olearski, Alison Roberts and Bernard Hayden. We were able to try the materials out at the Cambridge Eurocentre and the Cambridge Regional College (where Anita Harmer's comments were also extremely useful). Thanks to both organizations for allowing us to get valuable feedback.

Lastly, and with feeling, our gratitude is due to Anita and Annick for their support and patience.

Jeremy Harmer
Richard Rossner

Cambridge. July 1991.

We are grateful to the following for permission to reproduce copyright material;

Adverkit International Ltd for an extract from an article from *Bath & District Star* 1.11.89; Faber & Faber Ltd for the poem 'Giving Up Smoking' from *Making Cocoa for Kingsley Amis* by Wendy Cope; the author's agent for an adapted extract from *The Truth About Lorin Jones* by Alison Lurie; the author's agent for the poem 'Worry' from *Melting into the Foreground* by Roger McGough (pub Kestrel Books); The Open University Press for an adapted extract from Unit 6 from course *D303* by The Open University (pub 1978), (c) The Open University Press; the author, Michael Swan for his poem 'Old Friend Seen on TV'.

We have been unable to trace the copyright holder in the article 'Your Horoscope' by Lucille Burton & would appreciate any information that would enable us to do so.

Thanks are due to the following for permission to reproduce photographs on the pages indicated:

J. Allan Cash Ltd: pp. 5, 76, 107 (bottom centre and top left), 116, 148–151, 153, 155(c), 159; Catherine Ashmore: p. 111(f); BBC: p. 94 (top left); Peter Cotton and Mark Harrison, Abacus/Sphere Books: p. 2; Peter Dazeley: p. 73 (top); Zöe Dominic: p. 111(b); ET Archive: p. 54; Format Photographers Ltd/Jenny Matthews: pp. 78(d), 111(c),/Maggie Murray: pp. 71(e), 73 (bottom centre),/Joanne O'Brien: p. 94 (middle right),/Brenda Prince: p. 94 (bottom left); Format Partners/Ulrike Preuss: p. 78(b)(e); Tim Graham: p. 111(d); Sally and Richard Greenhill: pp. 34 (main photo), 37, 43, 61(a)(d), 73 (bottom left), 78(c), 94 (middle left and bottom right) 107 (bottom right); Robert Harding Picture Library Ltd: p. 107 (top centre); The Image Bank: pp. 139, 152; Japan National Tourist Organisation: p. 71(a); Mary Evans Picture Library: p. 157; Dept. of Medical Illustration, St. Bartholomew's Hospital: p. 118; Network Photographers/Sunil Gupta pp. 57(d), 94 (top right); Photofusion/Anna Arnone: pp. 57(b), 71(c),/Janis Austin: pp. 57(a)(e), 107 (bottom left), 145(d)/Vania Coimbra: p. 71(d),/Gina Glover: p. 107 (top right),/Sally Lancaster: pp. 57(f), 145(b),/Sarah Saunders p. 63 (bottom right),/J. Southworth: p. 63 (top right),/Sarah Wyld p. 145(a)/Vicky White: p. 78(a); Popperfoto: pp. 71(b), 111(e); Walter Rawlings: p. 34 (inset); Rex Features Ltd: pp. 15, 61(b), 73 (bottom right), 101, 145; Chris Ridgers: p. 141; Roose and Partners: p. 78(f); Syndication International: pp. 57(c), 61(c); Zefa: p. 52, - K+H Benser: p. 63(a), - Norman: p. 111 (bottom left); - Stockmarket: p. 63 (top left), - Teasy: p. 85.

Introduction for students and teachers

AIMS

The aims of **More than Words** are:

a) to make students more aware of words and what it means to know and use words fully (especially in English).

b) to make students aware of the vocabulary associated with certain defined topic areas (e.g. health, sleeping and waking, clothing, feelings and moods, relationships, character etc.): to provide material to help students memorize and practise these words.

c) to provide material which will provoke and stimulate, thus enabling the students to understand more about the vocabulary of English and how language works.

d) to provide material which can be used to promote general skill integration work and other types of language study.

THE ORGANIZATION OF **MORE THAN WORDS**

There are two books in the 'More than Words' series. Each book has Part A and Part B.

This is what the different parts contain:

BOOK 1

Part A: Exploring Vocabulary
12 units designed to help the students develop an awareness of different aspects of meaning such as metaphor, collocation etc. and of how words are used. In the units we also look at how words can be changed and how they behave grammatically.
Part B: Human Beings
16 units covering people and human experience. We look at the vocabulary associated with the body, health, movement, the mind, perception, likes and dislikes, character etc.

BOOK 2	Part A: Resources for Vocabulary Development
	6 units dealing with the resources which students can use to help them develop their own vocabulary; two deal with dictionary use and there is a unit on how to remember new words. Other units deal with 'circumlocution', wordbuilding and creative vocabulary.
	Part B: The World
	25 units covering topic areas concerned with the world we live in. We look at the vocabulary associated with families, communication, politics, homes, towns and cities, education, crime, the environment, the animal kingdom etc.

WHAT IS VOCABULARY?

A glance at the contents list of **More than Words** will show you that there is more to the book than simply a list of topics and the words associated with them.

To know a word fully you need to be aware of many things, for example

a) you need to know what a word means (let's take the word '*dream*')

b) you need to know how it is connected to other words which mean similar things (e.g. *nightmare*)

c) you need to know what other meanings it can have (e.g. "*I never dreamt I could be so happy*" "*He's always daydreaming*" "*I wouldn't dream of it*" etc.)

d) you need to know how the word changes depending on its grammar (e.g. she was *dreaming*, she *dreamt*)

e) you need to know the grammar of the word (e.g. you dream *of* or *about* something)

f) perhaps, most importantly, you need to know what kind of situations the word is used in and who might use it.

All this information is part of 'knowing' a word: it's information that speakers of the language have without even realizing it.

In **More than Words** we try to ensure that students have a chance to know words in this way. Texts show the contexts words are used in, and exercises explore various aspects of the words such as collocation, style and grammar.

A major feature of **More than Words** is *Part A: Exploring Vocabulary*, where students are made aware of what is involved in 'knowing' a word fully.

Part A can also be used as a reference section by students working on a unit in *Part B*. Some exercises have headings which refer students back to the relevant part of *Part A*, e.g.

MEANING

Part A Unit 1

CHOOSING A UNIT

More than Words is designed to be used in a number of different ways. Teachers and students should decide together which parts of the book they wish to use and which order they want to do them in. Here are some suggestions:

a) Choose units from *Part B*. If difficulties occur (e.g. with word formation exercises) refer back to the relevant section of *Part A* (Units 7 – 9) for clarification.

   The students and teacher may decide to do only one unit. If they want to do more than one, however, it is worth looking at how related units can be grouped together e.g.

   Example 1:

Unit 4	Health and exercise
Unit 5	Sickness and cure

   Example 2:

Unit 6	Ages and ageing
Unit 7	Birth and death

   Example 3:

Unit 11	The mind and thinking
Unit 12	Perception and the senses
Unit 13	Feelings and moods
Unit 14	Likes and dislikes

b) Choose the units in *Part A* that would be the most useful. Do them and then go on to *Part B*.

   Example: The teacher and students have decided that they are particularly worried about collocation – a frequent area of difficulty for this group. They would also benefit from discussing parts of speech and they have trouble with spelling.

This will be their programme:

Part A:	1 Meaning in context (as an introduction)
	5 Collocation – which word goes with which?
	7 Parts of speech: verbs and nouns
	9 Spelling and sounds
Part B:	Units 1 – 2

c) Work through *Part A* and then choose some units from *Part B* (see (d) below)

d) Work through *Part A* and then work through *Part B*

WHAT THE UNITS CONTAIN

PART A

1 Units in *Part A* usually start in one of two ways:

a) **With a text:** this is used to introduce a topic, but more importantly it is used to
   – demonstrate words in context
   – be a resource for students and teachers to use as they complete the awareness activities in the unit

b) **With a language question:** students might be asked to think of the different meanings of certain words, to identify parts of speech, to match up words which go together etc.

2 Exercises in *Part A* include the following:
   – matching exercises
   – filling in blanks
   – filling in charts
   – activation exercises designed to allow students to use the words or concepts they have been looking at.
   Depending on the size of the class, these exercises can be done by the teacher working with all the students or by the students working in pairs or small groups. Unless otherwise stated, the students should always have access to a good monolingual learner's dictionary.

PART B   Units in *Part B* follow a pattern consisting of three parts

> ENGAGE

> STUDY

> ACTIVATE

1 *Engagement activities*

These are activities designed to engage the interest of the students in the topic and its related vocabulary. Engagement activities will usually consist of one of the following:

a) **A text:** students are asked to read a text and then react to it in some way. It may lead to a discussion or a task. The purpose of the text is to arouse the students' interest as well as to introduce the vocabulary and concepts which are to be studied later. It is also there to provide a focus for general integrated skill work.

b) **A discussion/interaction:** For example, students complete a questionnaire working in pairs. It contains words and concepts to be used in the unit. Students discuss their opinions or compare information about a topic. These exercises provide an opportunity for students to consider topics in the light of their own experience . . .

c) **A word task:** students do a straightforward matching activity as a way of introducing the topic area and giving them the information they need for a discussion/interaction.

Almost all of these engagement activities are designed for use in pairs or groups. Students should be encouraged to participate as fully as possible.

2 *Study activities*

The study activities are designed to explore the words which the topic has introduced in more detail. Some of these activities are:

a) **Completing charts:** students are often asked to complete a chart. If the focus is on word formation it might look something like this:

adjective	noun	adverb	verb
loving	love	*lovingly*	love

If the focus is on which words go together it might look something like this:

	homework	the beds	the washing up	supper
do	✓		✓	
make		✓		✓

b) **Fill-ins:** students are frequently asked to fill in the blanks in sentences or paragraphs using words that they have been studying. Sometimes they are asked to select the correct word from a box. Sometimes they are asked to select a word and use the correct form (e.g. adjective, noun etc.) in the blanks.

c) **Matching:** students are asked to match one set of things with another. It might be a set of words with a set of pictures, e.g. The verbs in the box have to be matched to pictures of different animals (e.g. horse, elephant, rhino, snake etc.)

> *canter   trot   hop   crash   gallop*
> *bound   slither   pad*

Sometimes words or expressions have to be matched with meanings, e.g. in the exercise below, students have to match the expressions on the left with the feelings or emotions on the right:

a) She's *as white as a sheet*
b) She went *bright red*
c) She *came out in goose pimples*
d) Her *eyes narrowed*
e) She was *wide-eyed*
f) She *pursed her lips*
g) She *gritted her teeth*

> *disapproval*
> *shock*
> *emotional excitement*
> *wonder*
> *fear*
> *determination*
> *suspicion*
> *embarrassment*

d) **Discussing words:** students are asked to discuss words and with the help of their own knowledge and their monolingual dictionaries they have to make decisions about them. For example; do the words *thin, slim, skinny* have negative or positive connotations? Does the word *pretty* refer only to women or can it be used for men?

e) **Searching for word meaning:** students are frequently asked to look for the meaning of words. This is done in one of two ways:

Students are asked to find words in the text, e.g.

Find words in the passage which mean:

a a suit of a kind worn by athletes, etc.
b informal
c items of clothing which can be worn together

Students are asked to use a dictionary to help them to be sure of the meaning of words, e.g.

Say when you might feel one of the emotions below. Use a dictionary to help you.

a unfriendly   e serene   i disappointed
b inadequate   f impatient   j intimidated
c guilty   g sensitive   k strong
d stubborn   h nervous

---

f) **Choosing between different words:** students are often asked to choose between two different meanings or two different words.

What is the difference in meaning between the following pairs of words?

1 i) I've been *sick*
  ii) I've been *ill*

---

3 Activate activities

The Activate sections in each unit are designed to give students an opportunity to use words which have been studied in the unit in a more creative way. There are many different kinds of such activities. Here are just four examples:

a) **Headlines:** students are asked to explain unusual headlines and write the stories which might accompany them, eg.

Widow Sues Hotel Cook

MIRACLE OF FIRST BABY FOR PANDA HING-HING

b) **Writing tasks:** students are asked to write descriptions, dialogues, advertisements e.g.

> Imagine that, having lost your sight or your hearing as a child of five, you have just had an operation that has more or less restored your sight/hearing. Write an entry for your diary or a short article for a magazine.

c) **Telling stories:** students are asked to use the words they have been studying in either oral or written stories, e.g.

> Tell the story about one of the following:
>
> **a** someone who went to the doctor and ended up in hospital by mistake.
> **b** someone who took too much exercise and lived to regret it.

d) **Commenting:** students are asked to comment on pictures and/or situations, e.g.

> Look at the photographs and complete the tasks:
>
> **a** give the people names.
> **b** give their ages and say what their occupations might be.
> **c** using adverbs as well as verbs, describe how the people usually walk.

4 How the activities interact

All the units in *Part B* start with an engagement activity and end with an activate activity. In between these two, the three types of activity in the unit (engage – study – activate) usually occur more than once. In other words students may do an engagement activity and then do some study exercises. Then they do a quick activate activity before doing some more study work. Or they may do an engagement activity, some study work and then do another engagement activity which will lead them onto a different track. This diagram shows some of the possible patterns.

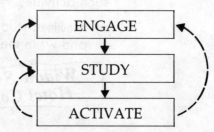

The material in the units can also be used for skills work, as a springboard for project work or for general language practice work.

HOW TO USE THE MATERIAL	The material in **More than Words** is designed for use in two distinct situations, classwork and self study.

CLASSWORK

Almost all the exercises in **More than Words** can be done by students working in pairs or groups. Indeed we believe that such interactions are a vital part of creating a healthy and cooperative class atmosphere. It is then the teacher's role to guide, advise and inform the students.

In small classes, however, the use of pairs and groups becomes rather artificial and in such cases there is no reason why the teacher and the students should not go through the material together.

It should be remembered that one of the teacher's main responsibilities is to encourage students to connect their own life experiences with the topic: that way lessons will not only be about learning language, but also about the topics themselves and how they affect us.

Some of the study exercises are clearly useful for students working on their own either in class or as homework. In such cases it is advisable to try to do the exercises before referring to the key.

In general we believe that the most important incentive to vocabulary learning is a feeling of involvement in the material on the part of the students, and it will therefore be a combination of the students' enthusiasm and desire to learn coupled with the teacher's encouragement of those attitudes which will make **More than Words** successful in the classroom.

SELF STUDY

While many of the activities in More than Words work well with groups of students, we have also tried to think carefully about students working on their own.

The most obvious way of helping such students is to provide an answer key which we have done on page 160. Students on their own can thus do the exercises and then check with the key.

The progression of the exercises associated with reading tasks etc has been designed so that students working on their own are still able to complete the tasks.

Obviously the more interactive exercises will lose something if they are done alone. Nevertheless questionnaires, for example, are still well worth reading through and thinking about, especially where they contain words which are to be studied.

Students working on their own should not forget *Part A* which clearly lays out the issues in vocabulary learning, speaking directly to the user/student.

DICTIONARIES AND DICTIONARY USE

One of the most useful tools for studying vocabulary at this level is the Monolingual Dictionary. In Book 2 there are two units which focus on details of dictionary use.

A good dictionary will give you lots of information about the words you are looking up. But be careful not to use it all the time, otherwise it will tend to get in the way of spontaneous communication. In **More than Words** we indicate where we think dictionary use may be appropriate by using this symbol:

CONCLUSIONS

More than Words is about vocabulary and how it works. It is about the words associated with certain topics. It is about language and how it is used.

We believe that words are fun and that finding out the strange uses which people have for them is an enjoyable task. Especially in a second or foreign language it is a voyage of discovery which will never end. We hope that **More than Words** will be a good companion on some of that voyage and that you will get as much excitement from using the materials as we have done from developing them.

Jeremy Harmer
Richard Rossner

PART

PART A EXPLORING VOCABULARY

Meaning in context

> *We often ask what a word means. It sounds like a simple question, but there may well be more than one answer. In this section we will look at meanings and how they work.*

1 In groups try to agree on what the following words mean before reading the text.

| trust   being single   galleries   biographer |

What do you think the text is going to be about?

2 Read this text. Disregard the words written as xxxxx.

Polly Alter used to like men, but she didn't trust them any more, or have very much to do with them. Last month, on her thirty-ninth birthday, it suddenly hit her that — though she hadn't planned it that way — almost all her xxxxx were now with women. Her doctor, her dentist, her accountant, her therapist, her bank manager, and all her close friends were female. She shopped at stores run and staffed by women, and when she had a prescription she walked six blocks out of her way to have it filled by the woman pharmacist at Broadway and 87th. For days at a time she never spoke to an adult male. When her husband left eighteen months ago, Polly hadn't expected her life to turn out like this. xxxxx and angry though she was, she had looked forward to the adventure of being single again. But as her friends and the media had already warned her, there weren't any good men over thirty in New York, only husbands and creeps. She'd refused to go out with husbands, and her other encounters had been such xxxxx that it made her laugh now to remember them, though at the time she had sometimes cried with disappointment and rage. After about six months she had realised she'd much rather stay home and watch television with her twelve-year-old son Stevie, or go places with her women friends. . . .

Three months ago Polly had had some luck at last: she'd been awarded a grant and given a publisher's advance for a book on the American painter Lorin Jones, born 1926, died 1969 almost xxxxx; now — partly thanks to her — becoming famous.

As it turned out, this commission had a striking, almost supernatural appropriateness. Though Polly had never met Lorin Jones, she'd been following in Lorin's path all her life. Lorin had grown up in a New York suburb; Polly (twenty years later) in a neighbouring suburb. Both of them went to school in Westchester; both, after college, lived on Bank Street in the West Village. Their xxxxx must have crossed, probably many times. When Polly was a toddler she and her mother might have passed Lorin and hers on the street in White Plains. Later when she began to visit galleries in New York, Lorin might have been among the other spectators; she could have been buying pantyhose at the same counter at Bloomingdales, or sitting next to her future biographer on the Eighth Avenue bus.

adapted from Alison Lurie *The Truth about Lorin Jones* (Abacus)

3 Answer these questions:

a What happened to Polly Alter on her 39th birthday?
b What is the connection between Polly Alter and Lorin Jones?

4 Which of the kinds of book listed in the chart do you think the text comes from? Why?

5 What are your reading tastes? Use the chart to find out what kind of books other people in your class like.

Romantic novel
Thriller
Detective story
Literary fiction
Humorous fiction
Biography
Autobiography
History book
Poetry
Other (please specify)

CHOOSING THE RIGHT MEANING IN THE CONTEXT

6 Write what you think these words from the text mean:

> therapist   look forward to   rage
> neighbouring   toddler

Check in a dictionary. Were you right?

So far the meanings have been fairly clear. But what can you do when you find a word you don't know? The simple answer is to think of all the possible meanings the word could have and then work out which is the most probable. Try exercise 7.

7 a Find all the words which are written as xxxxx.
b Write all the words that you think would be possible in the five places.
c Compare your words with your neighbours' in groups.
d Agree on one word for each xxxxx.
e See if your word is the same as the original. (The words are on page 160). If it isn't, check the dictionary meaning of the words on page 160 and see if your word means the same.

ACTIVATE

8 Work with a partner to act out an interview with Polly Alter. Take it in turns to play the part of the interviewer and of Polly. Ask her:

a how she gets on with men
b how she gets on with women
c what she is doing now
d how she feels about being single

Use vocabulary from the text.

9 Complete the following questionnaire with your neighbour.

Men and Women:
Which sex do you trust most?

For each question tick the correct column.

	male	female	both/either
1 Sex of interviewee.			
2 Which sex do you prefer the following people to be?			
your hairdresser			
your dentist			
your doctor			
a nurse			
a bank clerk			
an assistant in a clothes store			
a taxi driver			
a waiter			
your priest			
3 Which sex do you prefer as friends?			
4 Which sex do you associate the following characteristics with?			
gentleness			
truthfulness			
tolerance			
courage			
strength			
logic			
assertiveness			
5 On your first space mission would you prefer your highly-skilled captain to be male or female? Why?			